A LETTER TO MY WHITE FRIENDS AND COLLEAGUES

A LETTER TO MY WHITE FRIENDS AND COLLEAGUES

WHAT YOU CAN DO RIGHT NOW TO HELP THE BLACK COMMUNITY

STEVEN S. ROGERS
HARVARD BUSINESS SCHOOL, RETIRED

WILEY

Published by John Wiley & Sons, Inc., Hoboken, New Jersey.
Published simultaneously in Canada.

For general information on our other products and services or for technical support, please contact
our Customer Care Department within the United States at (800) 762-2974, outside the United
States at (317) 572-3993 or fax (317) 572-4002.

Wiley publishes in a variety of print and electronic formats and by print-on-demand. Some
material included with standard print versions of this book may not be included in e-books or in
print-on-demand. If this book refers to media such as a CD or DVD that is not included in the
version you purchased, you may download this material at http://booksupport.wiley.com. For more
information about Wiley products, visit www.wiley.com.

Library of Congress Cataloging-in-Publication Data is Available.

ISBN 9781119794776 (Hardback)
ISBN 9781119794806 (ePDF)
ISBN 9781119794783 (ePub)

Cover Design and Image: Wiley
Cover Image: © Photoco/Getty Images

SKY10025675_041421

Contents

Preface: Social Unrest, Protests, and the Podcasts

Breonna Taylor Was Shot and Killed by Police in Her Own Home[1]

(March 13, 2020)

Ahmaud Arbery: Father and Son Charged with Murder of US Black Jogger[2]

(February 23, 2020)

George Floyd's Death Was Murder[3]

(June 24, 2020)

LISTED ABOVE ARE what I consider to be the three most descriptive newspaper headlines in 2020. Each captures the incidents that were the catalysts for the country's racial, social unrest, and protests, known collectively as the Black Lives Matter movement.

George Floyd was murdered by a cop who put his knee on George's neck for 8 minutes and 46 seconds on May 25, 2020. Six days later, amidst the continuous protests and social unrest in the country, my youngest daughter, Ariel, 32 years old, sent me the following text:

Dad,

I think you should do a podcast as if you were the President. Something to provide a voice and some guidance to Black people right now regarding how to push forward. What to do with the emotion we all feel stuck with, to acknowledge that White people will likely disappointingly, try to keep going about the day today in a "business as usual" manner. We need you to keep encouraging us to respect COVID and its potential fatality. Equally important is that we need you to encourage Black folks to take care of ourselves which means:

A. It's okay to cry. This is sad and heartbreaking. We have to honor our emotions.
B. Be prepared to persevere and keep fighting the good fight. Actively protest if you feel like taking to the streets will help positively give the pain into something.

Dad, whatever your message would be, I know that it can be incredibly impactful!

It is this heartfelt plea from Ariel, who is a former executive salesperson with a fintech company, with a degree in engineering from Princeton University and an MBA from Northwestern University's Kellogg School of Business, that led to my production of the podcast "Say It Loud! I'm Black and I'm Proud. . .and I'm Angry and Hurting" The targeted audience was Black Americans. Here is the podcast in its entirety:

Say it loud, I'm Black, and I'm proud. . . .and I'm angry and I'm hurting!

For those of you too young to know, the first 8 words that I just mentioned were from a song written by James Brown, 52 years ago, and the last sentence that I just mentioned was from my daughter, Ariel Rogers, two days ago. All of my previous podcasts have focused on Black businesses. This podcast will focus on the business of helping Black America after a month of Black murders by White men.

I am not going to use this platform to tell Black people to vote, that I have heard advised by Black politicians and entertainers. I do not believe there is any value at this time to tell Black people to suppress their anger and hurt until the voting booths open in November. My advice is that Black people should be authentic and own these feelings. Continue to march and protest. You are going through the multi-step grieving process. Do not let anyone hoodwink you into trying to skip important steps in the process of grief when a Black man has been lynched by a White cop!

My friends, I still hurt and grieve from hearing, as an 11-year-old, my mother crying in her bedroom: 52 years ago, when the news reported that Dr. Martin Luther King Jr. had been murdered.

I still hurt and grieve from attending a church service at Mother Emanuel Church in Charleston, South Carolina, 100 days after a White man murdered nine Black parishioners doing a prayer service meeting in 2015. And I still hurt and grieve from the photo I saw of a Black family, a father, a mother, and two children, lynched, hanging from a tree by their necks, when I visited the lynching museum last year in Montgomery, Alabama.

Therefore, I come to you with shared anger and grief experiences. Own it. Do not let someone tell you that you're wrong for owning and displaying these natural feelings! In addition to that advice, let me give you some more constructive advice:

1. *Please let yourself cry. These are horribly sad times for Black people. Let your true emotions and feelings out. Remember,*

crying is not a sign of weakness. It is a sign of humanity, a sign of civility, and a sign of strength.

2. *Keep fighting the good, peaceful fight. No positive change has ever happened for Black people without major disruption.*
3. *Love yourself and love the Black community.*

In closing, be good to yourself. You are the descendants of strong Black men and women who survived the Middle Passage. This is our country, too. You are young, gifted, and Black. And as a result of your participation in marches and protests, when your slave ancestors ask you 50 years from now when you enter heaven, "What did you do for our people when you were free?" you want to be able to say, "I stood up and demanded from White America justice and humane treatment, as I proudly proclaimed, 'Black Lives Matter!'"

During this time, many Black people were so angry, frustrated, and exhausted that when their White friends asked, "What can I do to make racial matters better?" many Black people responded with exasperation, "Don't ask me how to help solve a problem that I didn't create! You figure it out!" This is a lost opportunity.

While I completely understand the irritation that led to this answer, as a teacher for almost 25 years, I knew this was a teachable moment. It is with this objective of teaching that I created a second podcast, targeting a White audience.

One of the highlights of that podcast includes the following statement:

"How can I help?" is a perfect question for the circumstances that we presently face. It reminds me of a story mentioned in the book The Autobiography of Malcolm X, *a book that* Time *magazine ranked as one of the ten most influential nonfiction books of the*

20th century. In 1960, Malcolm X was on a college tour giving speeches about the country's anti-Black practices and government policies. After one of his speeches, a young White woman approached him and asked, "What can I do?" Malcolm replied, "Nothing," and walked away. He later said that his response was a major regret, that he should have used the occasion as a teachable moment that could have resulted in the young woman using her financial and other resources to help the Black community.

This lesson that I learned from Malcolm X, about working with people who want to help the Black community, is the reason that I have written this book. My community needs your help.

Notes

1. Read, Bridget. "Breonna Taylor Was Shot and Killed by Police in Her Own Home." Thecut.com. March 13, 2020, last modified September 29, 2020. https://www.newsbreak.com/news/1595603620168/breonna-taylor-was-shot-and-killed-by-police-in-her-own-home
2. "Ahmaud Arbery: Father and Son Charged with Murder of US Black Jogger." BBC.com. May 8, 2020. https://www.bbc.com/news/world-us-canada-52585505
3. Parks, Brad. "George Floyd's Death Was 'Murder' and the Accused Officer 'Knew What He Was Doing' Minneapolis Police Chief Says." CNN. June 24, 2020. https://www.cnn.com/2020/06/24/us/minneapolis-police-chief-comment-george-floyd-trnd/index.html

Introduction

Dear White friends and colleagues,

I have never written to you before, but I am doing so now because the country, and specifically the Black community, needs your help. There is a cancer in our country that keeps resurfacing over and over. That cancer is the government public policies that have worked to create and maintain the disparity between Black and Whites in all areas of their lives, including perpetuating the wealth gap. In response to these cancerous policies, we see protests and civil unrest, which are akin to chemotherapy being administered to fight a cancer. There is much that Whites can do to unravel the harm of these policies. In the finance arena, the only real cure for America is the elimination of this wealth gap, which would make the Black community as healthy, safe, and self-sufficient as the White community.

Therefore, I am asking individuals to redress the problem primarily created by the government but that benefits White Americans. Your help is needed in the form of wealth sharing. I am not talking about a penalizing redistribution of wealth. I am recommending a wealth sharing that happens organically and intentionally via commerce, investments, savings, philanthropy, and government policy. This includes:

1. Spending money with Black-owned businesses.
2. Donating money to historically black colleges and universities (HBCUs).
3. Depositing money in Black-owned banks.
4. Supporting reparations.

I strongly believe that these means will eliminate the wealth gap and finally address fundamentally our country's racial problems practically and substantively.

My concern comes from my familial devotion to the improvement of the Black community and is the reason why I wrote this book that focuses on solutions to the problem of wealth disparity between Black and White Americans. It is my belief that until this problem is addressed in a systematic way, similar to the systemic anti-Black practices and policies that are its root causes, that the social unrest will continue. If peaceful coexistence is to exist between Blacks and Whites, the wealth gap, where the average White person has a net worth of $170,000 compared to $17,000 for the average Black person, must be eliminated.[1] This gap does not exist because Whites are smarter than Blacks, nor does it exist because Whites save more than Blacks or have worked harder than Blacks. These commonly held beliefs are falsehoods of mythic proportions, refuted by objective empirical research.[2]

The reason for the racial wealth gap is simple, but barbaric. One scholar noted that slavery is the primary reason why Blacks hold 1% of the country's wealth today, compared to ½% immediately after slavery ended in 1865.[3] It stretches back to the moment those 20 abducted Black Africans were dragged to our shores in

1619, only 15 years after the first settlers landed in Jamestown, Virginia, in a ship called the *White Lion*. For 246 years, there were over 12 generations of zero wealth accumulation for Blacks, compared to the accumulation of hundreds of billions for Whites. The financial benefits to Whites were best described by a Duke University professor, Peter Wood, who said, "Slavery it seems to me was an extraordinary goose that laid the golden egg. . . . You had workers that you didn't have to pay, and you owned their children as soon as they were born. It's a preposterous system."[4]

American slavery was such a pervasive system in its enslavement and treatment of Blacks that financial wealth inured to the benefit of Whites whether an enslaved Black was alive or dead. Specifically, the financial benefits of enslaving Black people was ingrained in the fabric of almost every industry in the United States, including insurance, education, and banking. In the book and the movie *12 Years a Slave*, we follow the story of Solomon Northup, a free Black man who was kidnapped and pressed into bondage. At a moment in the narrative when Northup was going to be lynched by a White employee on the plantation where he lived, a bank mortgage ended up being a primary reason why his life was spared. Another White plantation employee stopped the hanging because killing Northup would have resulted in the bank expecting immediate repayment of a $400 loan. Northup's Black life mattered only because a bank was owed money.

When we think of mortgages, we imagine banks providing loans to buy inanimate assets such as real estate, but during slavery, the White banking industry expanded their mortgage portfolios by providing loans to buy Black people as well as issuing new loans using Black enslaved people as collateral to buy more Black people. This is similar to a homeowner who owns her home free and clear getting a new mortgage. Therefore, banks in the north and south made more profits from mortgages on human beings than on real estate.

Historian Bonnie Martin found that in some states, there were periods when slaves served as partial collateral for more than 80% of all loans.[5] At one time in Louisiana, the frequency with which owners used enslaved Blacks as collateral for loans approached 90%.[6]

Those men and women who did not escape death, like Northup, still had value. For example, it has recently been discovered that major medical schools used the corpses of Black enslaved people for research, anatomy classes, and dissection. This was called the "domestic cadaver trade" and participating schools included Harvard University, the University of Maryland, the University of Pennsylvania, and the University of Virginia. The prices paid for the cadavers, as reflected in the records of the schools that kept payment schedules, was $12 for adults, $15 for mothers and their infants, and $8 for children between the ages of 4 and 10. Often, these bodies were stolen from cemeteries.[7]

Another industry that profited from deceased Black enslaved people was the insurance industry. It was common for insurance companies to provide coverage to slave owners and slave ships. In the book *Zong!* by Canadian writer M. NourbeSe Philip, the author extrapolated from legal documents that 150 Africans on one slave ship were purposely drowned, so that the owners could collect insurance monies for the loss.[8]

Over 78 years after this horrific terminal fraud, Cudjo Lewis was reported to have been one of the last Africans transported to America as an enslaved man. He was one of the enslaved people on a ship called the *Clotilda*, which arrived in America in 1859, 50 years after the federal government had abolished the slave trade in this country.[9] This was a federal crime.

After the human cargo of 110 Black men and women departed the ship, it was purposely burned and sunk. The Meaher family, who had financed the illegal kidnapping, had the ship destroyed so as not to retain evidence of their crime. But in 2019, the ship was discovered in the murky waters of Montgomery, Alabama, not far from where Lewis had deboarded 60 years earlier.[10]

After almost two and a half centuries of his people being held in bondage and working with no compensation, generation after generation, this is what Lewis said when informed that he was free, and no longer an enslaved man owned by Tim Meaher and his family:[11]

> It April 12, 1865. De Yankee soldiers dey come down to de boat and eatee de mulberries off de trees. Den dey see us and say, "Y'all can't stay dere no mo'. You free, you doan b'long to nobody no mo. Oh, Lor'! I so glad. We astee de soldiers where we goin'? Dey say dey doan know. Dey told us to go where we feel lak goin', we ain' no mo' slave.

Afterwards, Mr. Lewis had the following discussion with Tim Meaher, his former slave owner:

> Cap'n Tim, you brought us from our country where we had lan'. You made us slave. Now dey make us free but we ain' got no country and we ain' got no lan'! Why doan you give us piece dis land so we kin buildee ourself a home? Cap'n jump on his feet and say, "Fool do you think I goin' give you property on top of property? I tookee good keer my slaves and derefo' I doan owe dem nothin. You doan belong to me now, why must I give you my lan'?

In 2020, on a segment on the television show *60 Minutes* about discovering the sunken *Clotilda* slave ship, it was reported that the Meaher family, descendants of "Cap'n Tim," owns land, businesses, and other assets worth over $26 million.[12]

This unwillingness to help the newly freed people, during what author Saidiya Hartman called "the afterlife of slavery" was a common refrain by individuals, as well as the government. Field Order No. 15 was issued in January 1865. This military order was intended to take 400,000 acres of land confiscated from confederate soldiers who were found guilty of treason and to disperse it to people who were formerly enslaved.[13] Unfortunately, President Andrew Johnson said this was advantaging Blacks over Whites and that it was time for Blacks to fend for themselves. In a speech he said, "It is earnestly hoped that instead of wasting away they will by their own efforts establish for themselves a condition of respectability and prosperity."[14]

We see that decisions refusing to share wealth, combined with the financial benefits of slavery going to Whites exclusively, generation after generation, is the foundation of the wealth gap between Blacks and Whites. This unbridged chasm started over 400 years ago.

Beginning as an enslaved people without the right to earn a living or accrue wealth from their work or to transfer any acquired wealth over 12 succeeding generations has left many of the country's Black Americans in a chronic perpetual state of poverty, making it almost impossible to generate financial independence or create a viable community economy to parallel that of White Americans. A perfect example of this disparity plague is the city of Boston, where a 2017 study showed the average White household had a net worth of almost $250,000 compared to a net worth of $8 for Blacks (the noted amount is not an error).[15]

Even more disturbing has been the reaction from Whites whenever there have been instances of Black success that could become the basis of wealth generation. One of the most prominent examples is the 1921 story of Tulsa, Oklahoma's "Black Wall Street" when a mob of White citizens destroyed the city's Black business community in a terrorist attack that witnessed the first aerial bombardment of American citizens on U.S. soil.[16] While this story of the destruction of 600 Black businesses is well known in the Black community, a recent survey by NBC news in Chicago reported that 94% of Whites had never heard of this event.

Racial inequities create systemic cracks in the structural strength of our country. They result in health issues, social problems, reduced happiness, and diminished economic growth. Wealth inequality is one of the roots of systemic racial problems, because wealth is a resource that provides the basis for financial security (short and long term) and political power. Wealth provides individuals, families, and groups with the power of mobility and a sense of agency because it is a strength developed across lifetimes and handed down through generations. And in addition to being a systemic issue, wealth inequality is a generational problem, undermining any foundation for the stability of the Black community, and for America.

How do we make America fulfill the dream first envisioned in Thomas Jefferson's Declaration of Independence? How do we reclaim the America that was betrayed in that great compromise of 1787, when the Constitution was created and excluded Blacks from a timelier participation in this great experiment? The solutions I offer in this book focus on seeking financial equity. Black Americans were officially excluded from wealth generation for 246 years through government-sanctioned slavery and over 100 years of other anti-Black public policies. Therefore, we need to take extraordinary steps – even more radical than what was true of affirmative action – to correct the wrong. As Nikole Hannah-Jones of the *New York Times* said, "All of this inequality was intentionally constructed. Therefore, all of it can be intentionally deconstructed."

So, what is the road forward? What can be done to undo the financial apartheid that has resulted in Whites having 10 times the net worth of Blacks? Just as Nelson Mandela and willing White Afrikaaners helped South Africa avoid social disruption that was broiling increasingly hotter in their country, we need similar leadership. I know that the problems include issues with the police, but my focus is on what I believe is an equally important cause of the protests, and that is the wealth disparity. Therefore, you, my White colleagues in the business community, are needed to help diffuse the pressures that drive the wealth disparities that contributed to the past riots and fuel the current protests that are breaking out with increasing frequency in 21st-century America.

To the White business community that asks, "What can I do?" please imagine that the current status of Black America is the result of a terrible wound. Therefore, the task here is to heal that wound, to salve the hurt from the blow. Even Harvard University is now asking this question about redemption as they publicly recognize the fact that enslaved Black men and women were forced to work on the campus as early as 1639. In fact, the names of four of those enslaved people were identified in a ceremony on campus in 2016. Congressman John Lewis was the keynote speaker. Four of those enslaved people were Titus, Venus, Bilhah, and Juba. They were owned by Harvard University presidents Benjamin Wadsworth and Edward Holyoke from 1725 to 1737.[17]

The recommendations detailed in the following chapters examine how we may heal the wound by eliminating the Black-White wealth gap. To that end, the chapters will:

1. Provide you with practical solutions on how you can help the Black community.
2. Help you understand how you can improve Black-White racial relations.
3. Teach Black American history that you likely did not learn in high school or college.
4. Identify some root causes of the country's race problems, because root cause analysis is key to determining solutions.

5. Help you empathize with the socioeconomic challenges experienced by most of the 30 million Black Americans who are not entertainers or athletes.
6. Teach that Black Americans are the most loyal and patriotic group of people in the country.
7. Teach that eliminating the $153,000 wealth gap between Blacks and Whites is the solution to an overwhelming percentage of our problems.

Sincerely, your friend and advisor,
Steven Rogers

Notes

1. Jan, Tracy. "White Families Have Nearly 10 Times the Net Worth of Black Families. And the Gap Is Growing." *Washington Post*, September 28, 2017. https://www.washingtonpost.com/news/wonk/wp/2017/09/28/black-and-hispanic-families-are-making-more-money-but-they-still-lag-far-behind-whites/
2. Darity, W. A., Darrick Hamilton, Mark Paul, Alan Aja, A. Prince, Antonio Moore, and Caterina Chiopris. "What We Get Wrong about Closing the Racial Wealth Gap." Samuel DuBois Cook Center on Social Equity at Duke University, April 2018. https://socialequity.duke.edu/portfolio-item/what-we-get-wrong-about-closing-the-racial-wealth-gap/
3. Baradaran, Mehrsa. *The Color of Money: Black Banks and the Racial Wealth Gap*. Harvard University Press, 2017.
4. "Slavery and the Making of America." PBS. n.d. www.Thirteen.org. https://www.thirteen.org/wnet/slavery/about/p_transcript2.html
5. Martin, Bonnie. "Slavery's Invisible Engine: Mortgaging Human Property." *Journal of Southern History* 76, no. 4 (2010): 817–866.
6. "Let Us Put Our Money Together: The Founding of America's First Black Banks." n.d. www.Kansascityfed.org. Accessed December 27, 2020. https://www.kansascityfed.org/publications/aboutthefed/letusputourmoneytogether
7. Berry, Daina Ramey. "Beyond the Slave Trade, the Cadaver Trade." *New York Times*, February 3, 2018. https://www.nytimes.com/2018/02/03/opinion/sunday/cadavers-slavery-medical-schools.html

8. Okeowo, Alexis. "How Saidiya Hartman Retells the History of Black Life." *New Yorker*, October 26, 2019. https://www.newyorker.com/magazine/2020/10/26/how-saidiya-hartman-retells-the-history-of-black-life

9. Keyes, Allison. "The 'Clotilda,' the Last Known Slave Ship to Arrive in the U.S., Is Found." Smithsonian. Smithsonian.com. May 22, 2019. https://www.smithsonianmag.com/smithsonian-institution/clotilda-last-known-slave-ship-arrive-us-found-180972177/

10. Raines, Ben. "Wreck Found by Reporter May Be Last American Slave Ship." Al. January 23, 2018. https://www.al.com/news/mobile/2018/01/alcom_reporter_may_have_found.html

11. "Zora Neale Hurston's Lost Interview with One of America's Last Living Slaves." Vulture. Apri 29, 2018. https://www.vulture.com/2018/04/zora-neale-hurston-barracoon-excerpt.html

12. Reeves, Jay. "America's Last Slave Ship Could Offer a Case for Reparations." AP News. October 5, 2019. https://apnews.com/article/1f0c197b0a1740aea9d6e34db3d28c6e.

13. Myers, Barton. "Sherman's Field Order No. 15." *New Georgia Encyclopedia*, https://www.georgiaencyclopedia.org/articles/history-archaeology/shermans-field-order-no-15

14. "Veto Message." The American Presidency Project. n.d. www.presidency.ucsb.edu. https://www.presidency.ucsb.edu/documents/veto-message-437

15. Johnson, Akilah. "That Was No Typo: The Median Net Worth of Black Bostonians Really Is $8." *Boston Globe*, December 11, 2017. https://www.bostonglobe.com/metro/2017/12/11/that-was-typo-the-median-net-worth-black-bostonians-really/ze5kxC1jJelx24M3pugFFN/story.html

16. History.com Editors. "Tulsa Race Massacre." August 6, 2019. https://www.history.com/topics/roaring-twenties/tulsa-race-massacre

17. Pazzanese, Christina. "To Titus, Venus, Bilhah, and Juba." 2016. *Harvard Gazette*. April 6, 2016. https://news.harvard.edu/gazette/story/2016/04/to-titus-venus-bilhah-and-juba/#:~:text=Affixed%20near%20Wadsworth%20Gate%2C%20the

CHAPTER ONE

Why Should You Trust My Advice? Who Am I?

ON JUNE 1, 2019, the *Boston Globe* headline read "At Harvard Business School, Diversity Remains Elusive."[1] The story was about my retirement from HBS, where I taught a course titled "Entrepreneurial Finance" and created a new course titled Black Business Leaders and Entrepreneurship in response to the absence of content about Black businesspeople in almost every course at the school. I left my alma mater in protest of this failing, frustrated and disappointed with its anti-Black attitudes and practices. Almost one year before retiring, I wrote a letter to Larry Bacow, the president of Harvard University. Here are some excerpts:[2]

From: Rogers, Steven

Sent: Wednesday, August 15, 2018 12:59 pm

To: Bacow, Lawrence S.

Dear President Bacow,

My name is Steven Rogers and I teach at the business school, where I am a Senior Lecturer. I have a pressing concern, but I'd like to begin with a short story:

On April 2, 1981, I was working as a purchasing agent at the North Carolina–based Consolidated Diesel Company (a $500 million joint venture between J.I. Case and Cummins Engine Company) when the plant manager told me he'd received a call from the director of the North Green Golf Club. The director informed him that I had lunch at the club, using the company's corporate membership, but in the future I would not be allowed to eat in the dining room because the club had a policy that forbade Black people from eating there. He said that if I wanted to dine at the golf club in the future, I, unlike the company's White employees, would have to eat in the kitchen where the Black workers ate their meals.

Two years later I began my wondrous relationship with Harvard Business School (HBS) as a student ('85), a member of the Visiting Committee (2002), and a faculty member (2012–).

Since arriving at HBS, I have taught entrepreneurial finance in our executive programs and created a new course, titled "Black Business Leaders and Entrepreneurship," which has enrolled students from 9 of Harvard University's 14 schools. I created this course after researching and discovering that our curriculum virtually did not include African Americans. Specifically, I learned that we had published approximately 10,000 case studies and only 60 (less than 1%) had a Black protagonist. I further learned that approximately 300 case studies were taught to our first-year students in the required curriculum and only 2 (less than 1%) had a Black protagonist.

It occurred to me that we were not teaching our students the full spectrum of business leaders. Our students were not being exposed to the business and leadership brilliance, as well as challenges, of Black men and women, many of whom had matriculated at HBS.

In an effort to quickly address this exclusion, I met with each of the 10 department course heads, shared my findings, and asked them to include at least one case study with a Black protagonist in their curriculum. I also offered to help them identify three Black protagonist candidates and they could select one whom they could include in a case study.

In response, virtually nothing was done. Therefore, I created my course and wrote 20 new case studies with Black protagonists to address this omission of Black businessmen and women in our curriculum. This was the first course of its kind – one that specifically highlighted Black business leaders – at Harvard or any other business school in the country.

This exclusion of Blacks in our curriculum, as well as Blacks in almost every area of the business school, is reminiscent of the bias against Blacks that I experienced in North Carolina. While there are no explicit anti-Black policies, the results are practically the same. There is an institutionalized racism at HBS that keeps Blacks out of almost every aspect of the school. It is virtually the same today as it was more than 30 years ago when I was a student. Progress in this regard at HBS has been glacial.

There are no Blacks in any position of leadership, including associate or assistant deans. There are only 2 Black tenured professors and less than 3% of the entire 300-plus member faculty are Black.

President Bacow, there is something terribly wrong at HBS. It desperately needs to change. It has a leadership and intellectual apartheid mindset that promotes Black exclusion and teaches our students, through its lack of racial inclusiveness, that qualified, brilliant, talented, and accomplished Black people are not important, nor are we worthy of fair and equal opportunities.

This school that I dearly love needs to change. True inclusion is not organic; it comes from purposeful leadership because it requires change and disruption. HBS's leadership is doing exactly the opposite: allowing the status quo to reign, which perpetuates the organizational norm of excluding qualified Blacks.

President Bacow, I hope that you agree that we can no longer afford for HBS to operate this way, and that a major overhaul is required if HBS is to truly be the greatest business school in the world.

Steven Rogers

The Anatomy of Race Men and Race Women

My departure from Harvard Business School was not a surprise to those who knew of my lifelong commitment to uplifting the Black community using the tools of business and, specifically, Black entrepreneurship. When I joined the HBS faculty, I told the dean that one of my objectives was to make HBS a significant and meaningful contributor to the Black community, locally, nationally, and internationally. The school's only impact up to that point was producing the same number of Black graduates that it produced when I was a student 30 years earlier, and most of those graduates went to corporate jobs, versus creating jobs for other Black people as entrepreneurs. This melding of business and uplifting the Black community is a powerful combination with huge potential impact on the latter.

I am proud of my commitment to the Black community, which led to the dean of faculty calling me a "race man." I was pleasantly surprised when she, a young White person, properly used that moniker to describe me because it was a badge of honor in the Black community that dates back to the late 19th century. A "race man" or "race woman" is "a Black man or woman who strongly advocates for the rights of Black people."[3]

Race Men and Women in History

There have been plenty of race men and women throughout U.S. history and continuing into the present, but there are a few whose impact on my personal and professional life has made me the person I am today.

Historically, a preeminent example of a race woman was Ida B. Wells, who publicly and persistently protested against the lynching of Blacks during the early 1900s.[4] Her brilliance and fearlessness as a journalist are reasons why Nikole Hannah-Jones of the *New York Times* and creator of the "1619 Project" called Ida her model. She lauded Ida B. Wells as one of the first reporters using empirical data to tell her stories, such as documenting and reporting the number of Black lynchings. The techniques that she introduced almost a century ago are still commonly used by journalists today. These innovative techniques of investigative reporting single-handedly turned lynching into a national concern. Her outstanding work as a newspaper owner and reporter was posthumously recognized in 2020 with a Pulitzer Prize.

My favorite race woman, due to her bravery, selflessness, and brilliance, is Harriet Tubman, a formerly enslaved woman. She escaped slavery and became known as "Moses" because she successfully and miraculously secretly returned to slave states thirteen times and helped other enslaved people escape. John Brown, the famous White abolitionist, called her General Tubman. She also served as a spy and leader of military expeditions in the Union Army during the Civil War, but never received a military salary. The pension that she ultimately received was from her husband's military service. She later donated land so that a senior citizens home could be built. She died at 91 years old. In 2016, the U.S. Treasury announced that her face would be put on the $20 bill, replacing that of President Andrew Jackson, an American president who owned slaves.[5]

Dr. W. E. B. Du Bois was one of the earliest race men in the country and the first Black American to earn a PhD from Harvard in 1895. The Du Bois medals are awarded to people who represent "Black Excellence" and are bestowed at a major ceremony on the Harvard campus every year, handed out by the famous Black scholar Henry Louis "Skip" Gates. Recipients include Colin Kaepernick, the NFL activist; Lonnie Bunch, the founder of the National Museum of African American History and Culture; Sheila Johnson, the co-founder of Black Entertainment Television (BET); and Robert Smith, the private equity investor who donated $40 million to Morehouse College.

Dr. Du Bois was one of the founders of the National Association for the Advancement of Colored People (NAACP), one of the nation's earliest and most effective civil rights organizations for Black people. Interestingly, many of the organization's other founders and leaders were White. They included Mary Ovington, Charles Russell, William Walling, and Moorfield Storey, the NAACP's first president. It is the spirit and actions of this kind, in support of the Black community by Whites, that this book implores White people to engage in today.

One of the most significant contributions of Dr. DuBois was to our current critique of Reconstruction, the twelve-year period following the abolition of slavery. This was the first time in

American history when racial equality was practiced and implemented nationally. Prior to his work, many American historians, politicians, and media argued that Reconstruction had failed because of the indolence and ignorance of recently freed Black people, rather than because of the failure of White society to continue its support of Black civil rights and the necessary and radical restructuring of American society.

Reconstruction was the vision of Abraham Lincoln and the Republican Party (which today is the Democratic Party) to establish the reintegration of the eleven Confederate states back into the Union and to establish a way to integrate Blacks into society as full citizens with equal rights. Reconstruction provided Blacks the ability to move about as they wanted, to get education, to own land, and to be paid for their work. The passing of the 13th, 14th, and 15th Amendments were among the strongest efforts the U.S. government made to support Blacks in this period, and, as a practical tool, there was the establishment of the Freedman's Bureau to assist Blacks in their transition to freedom.

During Reconstruction, another group of race men emerged. These were the first Black elected politicians, including Sen. Hiram Revels, Rep. Benjamin Turner, Rep. Robert DeLarge, Rep. Josiah Walls, Rep. Joseph Rainey, and Rep. Robert Elliott to the U.S. Senate and House of Representatives. Yet the backlash in the South was almost immediate. As the old elements of the Confederacy regained their positions of economic and political prominence, there rose the open and violent assault on the gains of the freed Black. When federal troops were withdrawn and control returned to White power interests, there was an increase in the use of violence, intimidation, and coercion against Black and White voters to support pro-White politicians and undermine the pro-Black political and economic efforts of Reconstruction. The systemic result of this terrorist campaign was the abrogation of all the political gains of Black office holders in the South. A prominent example was Wilmington, North Carolina, in the last decade of the 19th century. Unlike the failed coup d'état of the U.S. government on January 6, 2021, the overthrow of the elected government in this city was successful.

After the Civil War ended, Blacks constituted the majority of the population in the city of Wilmington. Under the aegis of Reconstruction, Blacks were able to parlay this into economic and political gains, electing three aldermen, a member to the Board of Audit and Finance, a justice of the peace, deputy clerk of the court, coroners, policemen, and mail carriers. They were professionals including business men and women, clergy, and teachers. They also owned a Black newspaper. In addition, Blacks were skilled craftsmen, including mechanics, carpenters, stevedores, plumbers, and painters.

As the economic, political, and social fortunes of Blacks rose, so too did the resentment of Whites in Wilmington. This resentment was not limited to poor Whites who competed with Blacks in the job market, but included wealthy Whites who saw Black political power voting against changes in the tax laws that would allow affluent Whites to pay less in taxes. Matters came to a head after the depression of 1892 when White Populists and Black Republicans joined forces to form the Fusion Coalition, a successful political alliance with a platform of self-governance, free education, and equal voting rights for Blacks. The Fusion Party swept the statewide elections of 1894 and 1896. The anti-Black response was the forming of the White Supremacy Club that, in 1898, enacted a coup d'état of the duly elected Fusion Party officials, with the killing of 60 to 300 Black citizens and complete destruction of Black businesses and Black homes. Effectively, these events in Wilmington paralleled those across the South and represented the end of almost all of the Black gains seen during and resulting from American Reconstruction.

Contemporary Race Men and Women

I have been asked numerous times if there is a difference between contemporary race men and women and those in the more distant past. My answer is that there are virtually no differences. As in the past, today's race people are female and male, old and young, formally educated and street smart, Black and White, and poor and rich. Furthermore, the impact of technology on race men and women is as important today as it was yesterday. For example, in terms of technology, the video of the murder of George Floyd on May 25, 2020, was instrumental in the public elevating of the leaders of the Black Lives Matter protests. The same can be said about Dr. Martin Luther King Jr. rising to civil rights prominence as a result of the videos shown on television of "Bull" Connor the Commissioner of Public Safety in Birmingham, Alabama. On May 3, 1963, he ordered the use of fire hoses and attack dogs on Black protestors, who were peacefully marching to demonstrate racist treatment of Blacks. This attack was shown on the nightly news throughout the country.

Black Race Men and Women The list below identifies the different categories of race men and women:
1. "Get in Good Trouble"
   Those who speak up (e.g., Rep. John Lewis)
2. "Show Me the Money"
   Those who invest/philanthropists (e.g., John Rogers Jr. and Mellody Hobson)
3. "Moving on Up"
   Those who build and create jobs (e.g., Valerie Daniels-Carter, founder of V&J Foods)
4. "Not a Handout, Just a Hand"
   Social service providers (e.g., Greg White, founder of LEARN Academy)

In today's world of justifiable unrest and protest, the most prominent race women are Alicia Garza, Patrisse Cullors, and Opal Tometi. They are the 2013 founders of Black Lives Matter.

Being a collegiate football player, my athletic role models were great Black athletes who were racially conscious, outspoken, and cared about the Black community. They included the 1968 Olympic track stars Tommie Smith and John Carlos, who famously raised black-gloved clenched fists overhead as the U.S. national anthem played, recognizing them for winning the 200-meter race.[6] Like Colin Kaepernick today, who took a knee on the football field,[7] they were protesting systematic anti-Black racism in America.

Another past great "woke" athlete was Muhammad Ali, aka "The Greatest," the most famous American boxing champion. After winning the light-heavyweight Olympic gold medal at the 1960 games in Rome, the 18-year-old returned home only to receive anti-Black treatment. It has been reported that in anger and disappointment, he threw his medal into the Ohio River.[8] At the time his name was Cassius Marcellus Clay, which was also his father's name. It was also the name of a White abolitionist who fought against the enslavement of Black Americans.[9] Muhammad threw the medal away after being denied service in a restaurant in his Louisville, Kentucky, hometown, because he was Black. The *New York Times* reported that Whites in Louisville comfortably referred to him as that "Olympic champion nigger!"[10]

At the height of his success, on June 20, 1967, as a conscientious objector, he refused to be inducted into the U.S. armed forces. He defended his stance against the Vietnam War this way: "I ain't got no quarrel with them Viet Cong. No Viet Cong ever called me a nigger," and "My enemy is the White people, not Viet Cong or Chinese or Japanese. You are my oppressor when I want freedom. You are my oppressor when I want justice. You are my oppressor when I want equality."[11] More recent Black athletes who were advocates for the Black community include Lebron James, Magic Johnson, and Naomi Osaka.

Naomi Osaka, who won the 2021 Australian Open, joined protests in Minnesota following George Floyd's murder, and boycotted the 2020 Western & Southern Open tennis match in protest of the continued genocide of Black people. "Before I am an athlete, I am a Black woman. And as a Black woman, I feel as though there are much more important matters at hand that need immediate attention, rather than watching me play tennis."[12] During the 2020 U.S. Open tournament, to bring greater attention to Blacks who had been killed by police, she wore seven different masks, one for each of her matches throughout the 2020 championship held at Arthur Ashe Stadium. After winning her second U.S. Open title, Osaka said that the masks were a way of using her platform to protest this form of injustice and to advocate the message that Black lives matter.[13] The following list presents the masks Osaka wore, in order, detailing the names of the individuals and their tragedies:

1. Breonna Taylor, killed by police in Louisville, Kentucky, while asleep in her apartment
2. Elijah McClain, killed after being placed in a chokehold by police in Aurora, Colorado
3. Ahmaud Arbery, killed by three White men who had pursued him while he was jogging near Brunswick in Glynn County, Georgia
4. Trayvon Martin, a teenager pursued and killed by a neighborhood watch volunteer in Stanford, Florida
5. George Floyd, killed by a police officer who kept his knee on Floyd's neck for 8 minutes and 46 seconds in Minneapolis, Minnesota

6. Philando Castle, killed by a police officer during a traffic stop in St. Paul, Minnesota
7. Tamir Rice, a 12-year-old boy killed by police in Cleveland, Ohio

In an interview after her match, an ESPN reporter asked Osaka, "You had seven matches, seven masks, seven names. What was the message you wanted to send?" Osaka responded, "Well, what was the message you got? The point is to make people start talking."

Magic Johnson, the Hall of Fame basketball player, proved after retirement that he was not only an athlete but also a race man. He created jobs for thousands of Black people through his entrepreneurial ventures that included Magic Johnson Theatres in 4 cities, 13 Magic Johnson sport health clubs, and over 25 Burger King restaurants. But one of his most impactful actions to benefit the Black community occurred in May 2020 when his company provided $100 million in Payroll Protection Plan (PPP) loans to Black and other minority businesses, to create jobs for Black and other minority employees.[14] This money was needed desperately to assist Black business owners trying to survive during COVID-19.

But at the top of my list of Black athletes who are race men is Lebron James, widely recognized as the "Face of the NBA." Unlike most other athletes, Lebron has contributed to the Black community throughout his playing career. He has not retired. He has participated in protests and contributed to Black culture in ways similar to those associated with the previously mentioned athletes and more. But not everyone has loved him for his outspoken support of the Black Lives Matter movement and other causes targeting the improvement of the Black community.

One of the significant, community-focused actions that Lebron has taken was his founding of the I Promise School in his hometown of Akron, Ohio. The school opened in 2018 and was partially funded by the Lebron James Family Foundation. As the *New York Times* reported, "The students at the school were identified as the worst performers in the Akron public schools and branded with behavioral problems."[15] As an incentive to academic performance, he also provides full scholarships to the University of Akron, so far for as many as 2,300 students.

White Race Men and Women   I have been asked if a "race man" or "race woman" can be a non-Black person. My answer is yes. In my experience, there are not many, but a perfect example would be Juliette Hampton Morgan, who died from the pressure of being a race woman. She was a public-school teacher and librarian in Alabama. She rode the public buses regularly where she witnessed the indignities heaped on Blacks by the segregated system. This Jim Crow system required Blacks to pay their bus fee in the front of the bus, then exit and enter the bus in the back door. One day, she witnessed a Black woman walking to the rear of the bus, and the bus driver drove off before the paying customer could enter the bus. Juliette pulled the emergency cord and demanded that the driver stop the bus and allow the passenger to enter. After that incident in 1939, she repeatedly pulled the emergency cords on buses when she witnessed mistreatment of Black riders. She also became a regular writer to the local newspaper attacking the discriminatory treatment of Blacks. In support of the Montgomery Bus Boycott in 1955, led by Dr. King, she wrote in the newspaper, "Are people really naïve enough to believe that Negroes are happy, grateful to be pushed around and told they are inferior? They may take it for a long time, but not forever."[16] This woman was fired from jobs after her letters were published, but she continued using the pen as her weapon. A cross was burned in her front yard, and her friends and some family members disassociated themselves from her.

Sadly, in 1957, she swallowed a bottle of sleeping bills that killed her. A letter laid next to her read, "I am not going to cause any more trouble to anybody."[17] In his book *Stride Toward Freedom: The Montgomery Story*, Dr. King mentioned her by name and highlighted her efforts to help the Black community. The public library in Montgomery was named the Juliette Hampton Morgan Memorial Library in 2005. The same year, she was inducted into the Alabama Women's Hall of Fame.

Another White race woman who deserves immediate induction into every Hall of Fame associated with the Black community is MacKenzie Scott, who has used her wealth to help HBCUs (historically Black colleges and universities). This remarkable woman donated $560 million to HBCUs in 2020; no other person has ever donated even 10% of that amount. Her $20 million donation to Spelman College was accompanied by a short message to Mary Schmidt Campbell, the school's president. It read, "You know what you are doing. You do it well. I am affirming that."[18]

Once, in a conversation about a White person being a race man, I was asked if the same was true of White clergyman John Newton. In the late 1700s he wrote the song "Amazing Grace," which is about his being a horrible sinner, then finding the grace of God and becoming an abolitionist who fought against Black slavery. However, I do not believe that he merits the moniker of race man because his sin was being a slave trader for seven years.[19]

Another White race man was Dr. Herman Geiger. I learned about him when he died at the age of 95. He had a fascinating love affair with the Black community. At the age of 14, he ran away from home to live with a Black family in Harlem. When he later became a medical doctor, he established medical clinics in poor Black communities in the South. With funds from the government, he "prescribed" food for families with malnourished children to be purchased from Black-owned grocery stores, and the bills were paid out of his pharmacy budget. In response to complaints that he was misusing funds, he said, "Well, the last time I looked in my medical textbooks they said the specific therapy for malnutrition was food."[20]

While Johnny Carson, the famous talk show host, was not known as a race man, he did something in 1968 that showed he cared about the Black community. Similar to 2020, it was a year when the country was filled with protests over the government's horrible treatment of Black Americans. As shown in the 2020 documentary *The Sit-In*, in response to the question "What can I do?" Johnny stated that he invited Harry Belafonte, the brilliant entertainer who was the first artist to sell one million albums and a well-known race man in Hollywood, to be the first ever guest host of the *Tonight Show* for a week so that Black politicians, entertainers, and civil rights leaders could voice their opinions and views to an audience of millions of predominantly White middle-class viewers.[21]

Belafonte had 25 guests, of whom 60% were Black, including the comedian Nipsey Russell; the "Queen of Soul" and multiple-Grammy winner Aretha Franklin, who was earning millions of dollars and using it to fund the Civil Rights Movement; and multiple-Grammy-winner Dionne Warwick. The 10 non-Black guests were all people with the public reputation of being socially conscious and supportive of Black rights, including the Smothers Brothers, a brother singing duo who went on to receive the George Carlin Freedom of Expression Award; Academy Award winner Paul Newman; and Senator

Robert F. Kennedy. The senator was assassinated later that year as he ran for president. Another guest who was also assassinated that same year, Dr. Martin Luther King Jr., said on the show, "The economic problem is the most serious problem facing the Negro."[22] It was also on that show that Belafonte asked Dr. King if he feared being killed.

The Makings of a Race Man

One of the most memorable days in my life, when I knew that advocating for poor Black people was my calling, occurred when I was 11 years old. It was April 4, 1968, after 6 p.m. I was in my bedroom and could hear my mother crying in her bedroom next to mine. She was watching the report on television that Dr. Martin Luther King Jr., a great man of peace and an icon to the Black community, had been murdered by a gunshot. It happened as he stood on the balcony of the Lorraine Motel in Memphis. I believe that every American should visit this motel, which is now a museum. The museum tour ends outside of the bedroom where Dr. King stayed, still in the condition that he left it. He was playfully admonishing the young Reverend Jesse Jackson for not wearing a tie as they were departing for dinner and a community meeting afterwards. The next day he was scheduled to lead a protest march supporting the city's Black sanitation workers who were on strike.[23] His last words were to his music director, Ben Branch, "Ben, play 'Precious Lord' in the meeting tonight. Play it real pretty."[24] This was one of Dr. King's favorite songs. The "King of Gospel," Reverend Thomas Dorsey, wrote the song while grieving for his wife, Nettie, who died after giving birth to their son. Dr. King never heard Ben Branch play the song, but legendary gospel singer Mahalia Jackson sang "Precious Lord" at Dr. King's funeral.[25]

On April 4, 2018, the 50th anniversary of Dr. King's death, I taught a class in my Harvard Business School course Black Business Leaders and Entrepreneurship. Here are the notes that I used in my opening lecture that day:

- Echol Cole and Robert Walker, 2 sanitation workers in Memphis, Tennessee
- Torrential rain downpour
- Took refuge in back of garbage truck
- Malfunctioned electricity, truck compacter turned on
- Cole + Walker crushed
- Memphis Dept. Public Works refused to compensate their families
- This led to 1,300 Black workers to walk off jobs
- They were paid $0.65/hour, which is $4.68 today, no overtime pay, no paid sick leave, injuries led to firing
- Created union to represent them
- As we think about great Black business leaders, many, like A. Philip Randolph, were leaders of labor unions
- Next 2 months these sanitation workers went on strike using massive marches to demonstrate their unity to be treated like a human
- In fact, held signs that said "I AM A MAN"
- On April 3, 1968, Dr. Martin Luther King Jr. flew to Memphis to lead the march supporting the union
- His flight had been delayed by a bomb scare
- But Dr. King refused to quit. He said, in support of sanitation workers, "What does it profit a man to be able to eat at an integrated counter if he does not have enough money to buy a hamburger?"
- That evening, he spoke to a crowd of Black citizens at the Mason Temple, where he said, "Like anybody, I would like to

live a long life; longevity has its place. But I'm not concerned about that now. I just want to do God's will. I've seen the Promised Land. I may not get there with you, but I want you to know tonight that we, as a people, will get to the Promised Land!"

- Less than 24 hours later, at 6:01 p.m. on today's date 50 years ago, as he stood on the balcony of the Lorraine Motel in Memphis, a single shot was fired, hitting Dr. King in his right cheek, breaking his jaw and severing his spinal cord.
- As he laid on the balcony floor in a pool of blood, Clara Ester, a young Black teenager who ran to Dr. King's side, said King's face looked relaxed – peaceful. There was a hint of a smile on his lips. His eyes were open as if he was looking to heaven!
- 1968 marked the death of the greatest living leader, outside of Jesus, that I have ever known!
- Today, we recognize the 50th anniversary of Dr. King's death!

As I spoke those final words, I could hear sniffles from some of the students in the class, as they, like me, shed tears. My words did not make me cry. I cried from the memory, a half century earlier, of hearing my mother crying achingly when her heart was broken by the murder of Dr. King!

After class ended, I sat in my car and listened to the great jazz singer Nina Simone sing one of her touching original songs, "Why (The King of Love Is Dead)." The lyrics and her beautiful voice soothed my soul:

Once upon this planet earth
Lived a man of humble birth
Preaching love and freedom for his fellow man
He was dreaming of a day
Peace would come to earth to stay

And he spread this message all across the land
Turn the other cheek he'd plead
Love thy neighbor was his creed
Pain humiliation death, he did not dread
With his Bible at his side
From his foes he did not hide
It's hard to think that this great man is dead
He was not a violent man.
Tell me folks, if you can, just why, why was he shot down the
    other day?

Williams College is where I found my voice for advocating for the Black community. As a freshman in 1975, I entered this beautiful, small, predominately White college of 1,800 students, with less than 5% Black students, and yet instantly knew it was where I was supposed to be. Williams College was a classic ivory tower, but it was a place where Black pride, learning, and activism was strong. It is also my oldest daughter Akilah's alma mater, and where I married my classmate and ex-wife, Michele, the day before graduation. Many times, after hearing my stories about Williams College, other Black people have asked, "Is Williams College an HBCU?" The Black Student Union (BSU) organization was filled with phenomenal upperclassmen and women who were great role models and leaders. At the top of the list was Michael Knight, a brilliant English major, a proud gay man who would become a professor of English at Williams College. Others included Debbie Gould, MD, who became Chief of Pediatrics at the Permanente Medical Group; and Clarence Otis. There have only been 18 Black CEOs of a Fortune 500 company in our country's history. Clarence was one of the 18 when he became CEO at Darden (NYSE), the parent company of eight restaurant brands, including the Capital Grille, Longhorn Steakhouse, and Olive Garden.

These BSU members and several other upperclassmen demonstrated a fervent commitment to the improvement of the Black community when they led the student takeover of the administration building as a protest for better treatment of Black students. The exhilaration that I felt from this experience, one month after arriving on campus, was surpassed a few months later when these same leaders gathered for an all-campus candlelight vigil outside the faculty dining hall where the school's trustees were meeting. We were there to demand that the school divest any stock it held that was related to South Africa, a country that practiced apartheid against its Black citizens.

These great experiences led me to become an elected officer in the BSU. This was an anomaly. Typically, Black collegiate athletes – at Williams or any other school – do not get involved as leaders in Black student organizations. I was a football player, but more importantly I was a race man. However, it was not difficult to have such a focus at that time at Williams College. In addition to the wonderful older Black student role models, there were Black leaders in almost every fabric of the school.

The residential junior advisors for my freshman dormitory (East College) were two brilliant, kind, and caring Black men. One was Bill Spriggs, now a professor of economics at Howard University and the chief economist of the AFL-CIO labor union. In addition to these dorm leaders, 25% of the young men who resided on the first floor of the East College dormitory were Black. They were Elliott Decrumpe and James Foy from New York, Michael Gadson from Connecticut, Garry Hutchinson (one of the editors of this book) from Washington, D.C., Herb Irvin (my freshman roommate) from Mississippi, and me. While Williams College had abolished fraternities in 1962, we created our own fraternal brotherhood called the "Men from East." As I write this book, 45 years later, we still interact almost daily via a "Men from East" group chat. Our group now includes a pharmacist, a psychiatrist, a healthcare executive, two attorneys, and a businessman/retired professor. We all proudly recognize that we are members of W. E. B. Du Bois's "Talented Tenth," and with that unofficial membership we are obligated to help improve the poor Black community.

Dr. Du Bois popularized the term "Talented Tenth"[26] because he believed that the most successful Black people had an obligation to use their success to help uplift the other 90%, those less fortunate Black people in the country. We, the "Men from East," first learned about this term when we took Black history courses at Williams College. We embraced the Talented Tenth responsibilities then, and even more so almost a half century later!

Other leaders who had an impact on me at Williams were the Black coaches of our intercollegiate sports teams, including football coaches Patrick Diamond and Clarence Thomas (not the judge!), and Bonnie Crawford, the women's basketball coach.

My path to leadership as a race man was further emboldened by the presence of Black faculty. These distinguished scholars included:

1. Dean Chandler – Chemistry
2. Dennis Dickerson – History
3. Melvin Dixon – English
4. William Exum – Sociology
5. Larry Neal – English
6. Charles Payne – Sociology
7. Gail Peek – Political Science

And finally, there were Blacks in other leadership positions, including:

1. Fatma Kassamali – Director, Career Counseling
2. Eileen Julian – Dean

All of these, and many others, helped create a nurturing environment in which to learn about the history and needs of the Black community. I loved my Williams College experience so much that, as an alum, I made a major donation to the school to create the Rogers Family BSU Scholarship for leaders of the organization who are receiving financial aid. I had to give back to the school that had given so much to me, as well as to help Black students who came from poor socioeconomic circumstances as I had. When I had interviewed at Williams as a high school senior, the director of admissions, Philip Smith, asked me what my plans were to pay for college. I cried as I responded, "My mother does not have any money. I cannot come if I have to pay." Mr. Smith then calmly said, "Steve, we are going to accept you and you do not have to worry about money." And he was right. I never worried about money. My financial aid package included scholarship grants, student loans, and campus jobs.

A Race Man in Business

There are few things more beneficial to the Black community than people being gainfully employed. The government, locally and nationally, is the top employer of Black people. In the private sector, Black-owned businesses hold that top spot. Therefore, throughout my 40-year professional career, I have always done as much as possible to support Black entrepreneurs. When they succeed, do well for themselves, and grow, they do good for the Black community. Black entrepreneurs create jobs, and the people who have jobs are self-sufficient, and self-sufficient people live in healthy communities.

My first opportunity to support Black entrepreneurs in a meaningful way was two years after I graduated from Williams

College. I worked at Cummins Engine Diesel Co. (NYSE) in Columbus, Indiana. Early on, I jumped at the chance to be a member of the team for a joint venture between Cummins and J.I. Case, in Rocky Mount, North Carolina. I was a purchasing agent, responsible for buying rocker lever assemblies and other components for the engines we were building. I also volunteered to be the director of the company's minority supplier program, with the primary responsibility of identifying Black-owned companies that could provide products or services to us. The company's leaders knew that our new, half-billion-dollar start-up had multiple stakeholders, including investors, employees, and the community. The latter was 70% Black. I knew that we had to do more than hire a couple of hundred employees. And we did! We wanted Black-owned companies to be suppliers and vendors, knowing they would employ Black workers. We also knew that this action could create greater wealth for the owners of these companies, which would be spent in and donated to the Black community. Finally, we wanted companies that provided high-tolerance components for the engines we were building to complement the usual food services and janitorial services companies. The reason we wanted suppliers of engine components to be Black-owned was because those companies could make higher profits.

One of those companies was Custom Molding Inc., a high-precision metal products company in Raleigh, North Carolina. It was owned by Franklin Delano Roosevelt Anderson, who was an HBS alum. Mr. Anderson was the best! He personified my definition of a successful businessman. A Black entrepreneur who loved the Black community, he was an outstanding businessman and role model. His company had strong profits that he deposited into a Black bank; he employed over 75 people, many of whom were engineers; and he was a major philanthropist to the Black community. Two of his favorite beneficiaries were Bennett College and North Carolina Central University. Both are HBCUs in North Carolina. The U.S. Department of Education defines an HBCU as "any historically Black college or university that was established prior to 1964, whose principal mission was the education of Black Americans, and that is accredited by a nationally recognized accrediting agency or association determined by the Secretary of Education."[27]

Along with Spelman College, Bennett College is an all-female HBCU. Bennett College was founded in 1873 by Albion Winegar Tourgée, a White attorney who litigated the landmark *Plessy v. Ferguson* case, in which the Supreme Court ruled that "separate but equal" public facilities, such as schools, were not in violation of the Constitution. When I first visited Bennett College, I saw one of the best slogans that I have ever seen in my life: "Where the girl you are meets the woman you become."

Mr. Anderson and his wife endowed scholarships, in his mother's name, to Bennett College women. He also donated $1 million to North Carolina Central University. NCCU is one of the few HBCUs that was founded by a successful Black American businessman, Dr. James E. Shepard, in 1910.

In my eyes, Mr. Anderson's monetary success was second to his contributions to the Black community. He is the businessman who has influenced me the most by personally living the template for success. I have adhered to that template since meeting him four decades ago. He wrote my recommendation to Harvard Business School after he told me, "Steve, we need young Black businessmen like you who care about the community to get an MBA. You don't belong in the corporate world. Go back to school so that you can become a Black business owner. Do not become a politician! Do not become a lawyer! You are made for business."

Those words resonated with me in 2004 when I met Charles Tribbett III, the managing director and vice chairman at Russell Reynolds Associates executive search firm. Charles invited me to breakfast and told me, "Steve, I asked you to meet because I think you would be a great candidate for a new opening I have been hired to fill. Given your commitment to the Black community, combined with your leadership and business experiences, I believe you would be great as the next president of the NAACP, replacing the retired Kweisi Mfume." I immediately thanked Charles for considering me. I was enormously flattered, but I told him that I am not meant to be the leader of a civil rights organization. I am a businessman whose calling is to help the Black community through business. My model was Franklin Delano Roosevelt Anderson.

Taking a Stand from Within

While I had a wonderful experience supporting Black entrepreneurs in Rocky Mount, this is where I had my first overt, blatantly anti-Black, racist experience. After relocating to North Carolina from Indiana, my family purchased a house 12 miles from the company's headquarters. The back deck of the house overlooked the second fairway of the Northgreen Country Club (NGCC). After closing the deal, the sellers, a White couple, and I stood on the deck discussing how great the house would be for my family. As the conversation was coming to a close, the husband said, "Steve, I am sad to inform you that the neighbors do not like the fact that we sold to your family. They came to the house to inform me of how disappointing I was to them for selling the house to a Black family." That unwelcoming bit of news was then superseded by the fact that after moving into the house we learned that the daycare centers on our side of town did not accept Black children. We found a loving, elderly Black couple who lived close to the headquarters to care for my daughter Akilah while my ex-wife and I worked.

Finally, shortly after I began working at the company, I heard rumors that the company had an agreement with the Northgreen Country Club (NGCC) that gave employees a 50% discount on membership as part of the company's corporate membership. Of course, this too was a perk only for the White employees because Black people were not allowed into the country club.

After hearing this rumor, I called NGCC and made an appointment to have a lunch meeting with a White salesman. When we arrived at the club for our lunch, the person asked who we were, and I told her "Steven Rogers," using the corporate membership number for the company. The maître d' excused herself, asking us to wait, while she went to speak to the manager. He came back, greeted us, and showed us to a table. As we walked through the room, I could see the eyes of the other patrons looking at us. I could also see the light smiles on the faces of the Black waiters. We had a delicious lunch!

I returned to the company afterwards and was told by the receptionist to go see the company's president, Ron Gratz. I went to Ron's office, sat down, and he informed me that he had received a call earlier from the manager of NGCC informing him that I had lunch there, and he wanted me to know that they have a policy forbidding Blacks from the club. And, in the future, if I wanted to dine at the club, I would only be seated and fed in the kitchen with the cooks, not in the dining room. After Ron completed his statements, I waited to hear his response. But I got only silence. I then responded, "Ron, I assume you told him to kiss your ass! Because we are a company filled with

Black employees and we expect you to treat all of our employees the same."

Disappointingly, Ron told me that he did not say anything remotely close to my comments. Instead he told me, "Steve, we are not here to cause any problems. We believe that with our corporate membership, we can impact change from within." I told him that I totally disagreed with his strategy, that it was naïve and disrespectful to the Black employees. Then I told him that he should withdraw the company's corporate membership until the Black employees and White employees had the same opportunities and were treated equally. He and I agreed to disagree. Afterwards, I wrote a letter to the Cummins president, Jim Henderson, informing him of Ron's poor leadership.

In contrast, Jim Shipp, the highest-ranking Black person at Cummins, heard about the incident and asked me to fly to Indiana because he wanted to take me to lunch. When I arrived at his office in Columbus, Indiana, he said, "We are dining at the Corporate Executive Country Club because I want Jim Henderson and all of the other White executives to see that I support you."

Soon after, I learned the Atlantic Coast Conference (ACC), comprising schools like Duke University, the University of North Carolina, North Carolina State, and the University of Virginia, was having their annual intercollegiate golf tournament at NGCC. That was 1982, the same year future NBA great Michael Jordan hit the winning shot of the game, giving his school, the University of North Carolina, the national college basketball championship against Georgetown University.

The evening before the first day of the tournament, my family and I erected huge signs in our backyard facing the fairway of the golf course, so that they were visible to all of the golfers. One sign read "rACCism," another read "Why does the ACC support racism?" and another read "Michael Jordan cannot play golf at the NGCC."

Our protest was covered by the *Rocky Mount Telegram* and the *Raleigh News & Observer* newspapers. It later received national coverage from *Sports Illustrated* magazine, which sent a reporter to cover the story and interview me in my backyard, where they landed a small helicopter to transport the writer, Jerry Kirshenbaum, whose article, titled "On the Wrong Course," was published the following year.[28] Here are some excerpts from the article:

> The Atlantic Coast Conference has exercised poor judgment in its choice of sites for its annual golf tournament. For the past four years the tournament has been held at Northgreen Country Club in Rocky Mount, N.C., an arrangement that has become the subject of a crusade by Steve Rogers, a Black man who owns a house overlooking the club's 2nd fairway. Angry over Northgreen's admittedly restrictive racial policies, Rogers has argued that the ACC reinforces discrimination by holding its tournament at the club. During this year's tournament he posted signs on his lawn that were visible to the golfers. One of the signs read: RACCIST.
>
> ACC Commissioner Bob James has reacted coolly to Rogers' complaints. In a letter to Rogers, James said that the ACC's deal to use the Northgreen course runs through 1986 and that "in the absence of some very compelling reasons, we would not feel justified in breaching the agreement. Certainly, we would not use the facilities if we thought Northgreen Country Club was engaged in racial discrimination, but we believe that this is not the case."
>
> Northgreen has never had a Black member, and some of its practices are clearly discriminatory. Rogers learned this firsthand in 1981 after availing himself of his firm's corporate membership by having lunch in the club's dining room. Rogers

says his boss later received a call from a Northgreen official who wanted to "refresh" him on the club's rules against Blacks eating in the dining room; the club official said that Rogers had been served only to avoid an incident.

The Nashville (N.C.) Graphic recently interviewed an unnamed Northgreen official who indicated that the club was "not ready" for Black members. The official confirmed Rogers' account of the club's reaction to the latter's having eaten there. "Our policy is, we don't sit Blacks in our dining room in one-on-one, two-on-one or whatever situations," he said. He also said he was certain that the ACC office "knew all about" this policy.

The refusal of the ACC and its eight member schools, six of which are state supported, to sever their ties with Northgreen is distressing. In effect, the ACC is supporting a facility that practices discrimination. It also happens that golf and other minor college sports are largely underwritten by revenues from football and basketball, sports in which Blacks play prominent roles. In the ACC, 75% of last year's starting players in basketball and 50% in football were Black. It's sad to think that those Black athletes helped support an event at a country club that practices racial discrimination.

A couple of weeks after that article was published, the ACC publicly announced that they would no longer play tournaments at NGCC as long as it practiced anti-Black racism. The decision was reported in a *New York Times* titled "Segregated Club Out as Golf Host,"[29] which stated:

Amid a growing controversy over its racially exclusive membership policies, Northgreen Country Club announced today that it was withdrawing as the annual host of the Atlantic Coast Conference golf tournament. The announcement, which made no reference to the club's policies or the stir they had created, came as A.C.C. officials were reevaluating the conference's agreement to stage the golf championship there. The tournament has been played at Northgreen every year since 1980 and was scheduled to continue there through 1986.

My company withdrew its corporate membership the same week. NGCC changed its policy the next year and admitted its first Black member. I received tremendous national support, including the following letter from the athletic director at Williams College, published in *Sports Illustrated* on August 1, 1983:[30]

ACC Racism

I applaud Steve Rogers' gutsy [and, now, successful] effort to raise the racial consciousness of the Atlantic Coast Conference (SCORECARD, July 4 and 25).... Your readers may be interested to know that Rogers was a fine offensive tackle at Williams College for four years on some very good Division III football teams. I'm gratified that a former Williams athlete was the one who called for an end to the practice of official athletic complicity with racial injustice.

My experiences in Rocky Mount showed me that change that benefits the Black community has to be intentional. We intentionally supported Black businesses, and fighting anti-Black racism at the town's only country club also took intentional efforts.

A month later, I left Rocky Mount to pursue my MBA at HBS. During the summer after my first year, I was hired as an intern at Urban National Corporation Ventures (UNCV), which was one of the largest Black-owned private equity firms in the country. The firm was founded because Black entrepreneurs could not procure investment capital from White private equity firms. Pointedly, the same story exists over 30 years later. Black entrepreneurs have received less than 2% of all capital invested by the private equity industry.

However, this was a wonderful summer internship where I learned first-hand the difficulties that Black entrepreneurs faced in raising capital. As previously stated, the challenge still exists today, and I published a note at HBS titled "Sources of Capital for Black Entrepreneurs," in which I gave recommended solutions to the problem after citing research that shows the problem is primarily rooted in anti-Black racism.

The Importance of Being a Philanthropist

At UNCV I also met Dr. Larry Morse, a brilliant Princeton-educated economist. When I joined the firm, he was also a new employee. Today, he and his partner JoAnn Price, both HBCU undergraduates of Howard University, own Fairview Capital, a private equity fund that was created 26 years ago to provide capital to Black- and other minority-owned private equity firms. They currently have over $6 billion worth of assets under management in four funds. I have always "put my money where my mouth is" by investing in Black businesses. I am an investor in all of the Fairview Funds and was one of the first investors in their first fund over a quarter century ago.

In the spirit of paying forward Williams College's support of me those many decades ago, I have endowed scholarships at Chicago State University (CSU) and Evanston Township High School (ETHS). CSU is located on the South Side of Chicago and has predominately Black students. Alums include my brother, sister-in-law, and three nieces. The scholarship is called the Ollie Mae Rogers Scholarship, named after my mother, who never attended high school. But my mother loved business and was a fierce feminist, both traits that I also embody. This scholarship sends her to college!

The ETHS scholarship was named after my former father-in-law, Hoy Early Johnson. He never completed eighth grade, but he was one of the hardest-working and kindest people that I ever knew.

I also served a four-year term as a college trustee, where I successfully encouraged the finance committee, with the help of board chairman Bob Lipp, the former CEO of Travelers Insurance, to select Black-owned financial firms to manage millions from our endowment. One of the firms was Ariel Investments, which gave market-rate returns to the college as well as helping the Black community. For example, the firm created a school, Ariel Community Academy, that teaches financial literacy and investing to children grades K–8 from a poor Black community in Chicago.[31] The founder and president of Ariel Investments are John Rogers Jr., and Mellody Hobson, both alums of Princeton University. They recently went public in a 2020 article titled "PRINCO Claims It Prioritizes Diversity: Experts Want Proof."[32] Mellody and John implored Princeton to follow Williams College by investing some of the school's $40 billion endowment with Black-owned financial services companies. Mellody explained their reason for speaking publicly:

> "Our perspective on this grows out of a love of Princeton. John and I are indebted to our university. We have been, you know, Princeton fanatics for our whole lives," she said. "We only wanted to continue to see it thrive in every way for generations to come."

One of my other great accomplishments while serving as a trustee was proposing that we help HBCUs in New Orleans that were decimated by Hurricane Katrina. That proposal led to eight senior student science majors coming to Williams College in 2005 from Xavier University, which had six feet of standing water in the library a week after the hurricane in August of that year. Other schools, including MIT, Harvard, Princeton, Boston University, and Bates College, did something similar with predominately White schools in Louisiana, including Tulane and the University of New Orleans.

I am a retired member of the board of directors for S.C. Johnson Wax Co., a private family-owned business with over $8 billion in annual revenue. Our most popular products are Raid, Glade, and Windex. One of my major accomplishments while serving on the board was introducing the company to Black-owned financial services firms and getting the company to hire several to manage some of our pension fund capital. One of the firms hired was Fairview Capital, which was given over $5 million to manage. Larry Morse is now the chairman of the board of trustees for Howard University and has donated $1 million to his and vice president Kamala Harris's alma mater.

Like Larry Morse, I take great pride in philanthropy. It is through these acts of donations that I had an extraordinarily unique experience. Twenty years ago, a very close friend, Greg White, also a race man with an MBA from HBS, began a program to help Black children from poor communities in Chicago attend private schools. Greg told me about one such young man, and I immediately agreed to pay his tuition. Later, Greg invited me and my family to his house for a cookout, where he wanted me to meet the young man. When my family arrived, my children went to play with the young man and other children. An hour or so later, Greg told the young man that he wanted him to meet Mr. Steven Rogers. He happily replied, "He's here?" Greg said, "Yes, you've been playing with his children and you saw him an hour ago when he and his family came to the house." The young man responded, "Mr. Rogers is a Black man? I thought he was going to be a White man who gave me the scholarship."

The boy's name was Antwaun Sargent, and he is now a successful art critic and writer who has contributed to the *New York Times*, the *New Yorker*, *Vice*, and more. He is also an alum of Georgetown University and has published a beautiful photography book titled *The New Black Vanguard: Photography between Art and Fashion*.

Greg now uses his MBA as the founder of Learn Charter School. Twenty years after its creation, the school now has 4,000 predominately Black students in 10 locations. Over 90% of the students come from homes in low-income communities. Three of the portfolio managers at Harris Associates, an asset management firm with $90 billion in assets, are major donors: Bill Nygren, Rob Taylor, and David Herro. These philanthropists are White businessmen who have donated several million to this wonderful school. It would be great if other portfolio managers would duplicate their philanthropic donations to the Black community.

I believe fervently that philanthropy to the Black community is one of the highest-weighted criteria to be a true "race woman" or "race man." For as long as I can remember, I have always committed to donate at least 10% of my annual income to organizations and causes that support the Black community. Some of those Black organizations include Fisk University, an HBCU in Tennessee; Urban Prep Charter School for young men from poverty-stricken communities in Chicago and where my daughter, Ariel, was a math teacher after graduating from Princeton University; St. Sabina Church; Second Baptist Church; the Black Ensemble Theater; Harvard University's Black Graduation; the Dance Theatre of Harlem; and public elementary schools in poor communities, including Parker Academy, where my sister-in-law, Donna Rogers, teaches first grade.

Over 10 years ago, I told Donna that I wanted her students, despite coming from the poverty-stricken community of

Englewood in Chicago, to have the same classroom experiences and resources as first graders in public schools in wealthy suburbs. Therefore, at the beginning of every year, she gives me a list of everything she wants for her classroom and students. I never vet the list. I simply buy everything on it, including computers, library reading room kits with floor rugs, children's desks and chairs, special books, and snacks. I also automatically pay for any field trips that she wants the students to have, including the rental of a bus to transport them, admission fees, meals, and so on. The only question I ever ask is "Are you sure this is enough?"

A few years ago, I began doing the same with the class of Nanyamka Patrick-Hinton, the first-grade STEM teacher at a different elementary school called Laura Ward STEM School. I get the greatest joy when I receive letters written in first-grade penmanship with beautifully colored drawings from these students.

The first act of philanthropy that I experienced was when I myself was a child in first grade. At that time, it was customary for us to have a midmorning milk break. A carton of white milk was $0.03, and a carton of chocolate milk was $0.06. It had to be paid in full every Monday morning. My family was on welfare, and my mother did not always have the money. If you did not pay for the milk, you had to rest your head on your desk during the break. I rested my head for a week. The mother of one of my classmates was visiting school one day. She saw me and others who could not afford milk with our heads on the table. For the remainder of the year, she paid for all of us to have a carton of cold white milk with a paper straw!

Being the beneficiary of the philanthropy of others is how I got to where I am today. I attended high school at Radnor in Wayne, Pennsylvania, an affluent suburb of Philadelphia. I was there via a privately funded program called "A Better Chance" (ABC). The objective of this program was to enable Black and other minority students from poverty-stricken communities to live in and attend public high schools in wealthy communities. From 1972 to 1975, I lived in a house, donated by the community, with 11 other students from across the country, 3 college resident tutors, and a family as resident directors. The founder of the program was Roger Steinharter, a vice-president at Girard Bank in Philadelphia. Despite our age difference of at least 30 years, Mr. Steinharter and I became truly good friends. We also had several other differences, including the fact that he was almost a foot shorter than I am, and that I am Christian and he is Jewish. But we both had a life-long commitment to the improvement of the Black community and also enjoyed laughs that nearly brought us to tears. He loved telling the story, and laughed loudly every time, about living in an all-Black community in Newark, New Jersey, when his oldest son, Mike, was born. In those days, following birth, all the babies were put on display in the newborn visiting room in order for the fathers to see their babies when visiting. Mr. Steinharter said he would proudly stand in front of the big window separating the babies from the viewers. When a Black father joined him to look at his baby, Mr. Steinharter would gesture to the entire room of babies, which had only one White baby and say, "I bet you can't guess which one is mine!"

In college, I served as the resident tutor for the program in Williamstown. As a business school student, I served as the resident director of the program in Wellesley, Massachusetts, and I have served on the national board of directors. But most of my monetary donations have gone to the program in Radnor, where I told the board that I will pay for anything they need, including new computers, a new kitchen, and a new roof.

Conversely, my philanthropy to politicians has been limited since I donated to President Obama's initial campaign for the presidency in 2008. I had met him for the first time at a golf outing fundraiser for Greg White's charter school when Greg assigned him to my foursome. I knew very little about him other than that he was an Illinois state senator, which is not a very highly publicized position in Chicago. Greg told me that I would like Obama because he could help the Black community. He arrived late and rode in the cart with Derrick Collins, who taught private equity in my entrepreneurship department at Northwestern's Kellogg School of Management and is now the dean of business at Chicago State University. The other person in our group was Al Sharp, who taught entrepreneurial finance at Kellogg and is now a senior partner at a private equity fund of funds. They provide capital to Black and other minority private equity funds. Al and Derrick are both alums of HBCUs from Morehouse College and Prairie View University, respectively. Both also have MBAs from HBS and University of Chicago, respectively.

When we got to the third hole, Obama told me that he wanted to run for the Senate. I jokingly responded, "You can't win a Senate position because you just got beat running for Congress by Bobby Rush!" We all had a brief laugh and continued to play.

When we got to the fifth hole, he again quietly approached me and said, "I am serious. I want to run for the Senate." I responded jokingly again. "You can't win the Senate with two African names! You should be like my daughters, Akilah and Ariel, with one African name!" We all again had a brief laugh and continued to play.

He again approached me on the seventh hole and said, "Steve, I know that you don't know me, but I am dead serious about running for the Senate." This time my response was "You are right. I don't know you. But I assume that Greg put you in my group because he knows that I support anybody who will help the Black community, and I assume that you will too. Therefore, what do you want from me? As you can see, I am a horrible golfer, and I am playing worse because you won't give me any peace! What can I do for you?" He said, "I want to run for the Senate, but I can't because my wife wants me to first clean up my debts from running for Congress." I asked him how much debt he had and he told me $8,000. "I don't know you," I explained, "but I am going to trust you are as interested as I am with helping the Black community, so I am going to give you $3,000, and you can get the rest by coming to Kellogg's Black Student Business Conference in two weeks and make your pitch. The conference agenda is already set, but I will ask the students to do me a favor and let you speak for 15 minutes before the formal agenda. Now will you leave me alone so that I can play golf?"

Obama spoke at the conference, and the auditorium was less than half full. I introduced him and told the audience that I had made a donation to his campaign. After he spoke, others in the audience also wrote donation checks, all of which I am sure totaled more than $8,000. After he became president and I criticized him for not doing more for the Black community, a magazine reporter told me that, in relation to the $8,000 debt that Obama had mentioned to me years earlier, he had invested $8,000 to his campaign and was repaying himself with my money.

Paying It Forward

Conversely, a donation that gave me a phenomenal sense of patriotic pride was when I volunteered to teach entrepreneurial finance to cadets at West Point. For 12 weeks, I flew to Newark, rented a car, and drove to the Military Academy in New York. I was reimbursed for my expenses. My cadet students asked why I chose to volunteer. I told them I have always felt that something like military service was missing from my life. I envied the fact that my brother, father, niece, and uncle had served. When I told them that my 96-year-old uncle, Ray, was a buffalo soldier, they proudly pointed me to the huge outdoor grassy field dedicated to buffalo soldiers.

An audience of millions probably heard about buffalo soldiers for the first time a few years later, on December 23, 2019, when the NFL's Minnesota Vikings recognized Uncle Ray's service to his country during a ceremony. The public announcer directed the audience in the stadium and the television viewers to turn their eyes to the 50-yard line. My uncle sat proudly in a wheelchair, flanked by active military officers from each branch of the military as the announcer informed the audience that he had served as a buffalo soldier, where he was awarded three bronze stars. He wore a jersey with 99 on it to represent his age. This allowed him to hold on to his youth for 10 more days until he celebrated his 100th birthday.

I learned about buffalo soldiers from my Uncle Ray when I was 12 years old. It was from him that I also learned that Black Americans are at the top of racial and ethnic groups when it comes to military patriotism. No other group of people have fought in more wars for America than Black Americans, who have fought for the country in every war since the Boston Massacre in 1770, where the first person killed by the British was a Black man, Crispus Attucks. And we have given this service despite not being considered full citizens until the Fourteenth Amendment was ratified in 1868, nearly 100 years after the country gained its independence in 1776.

The 1948 passage of the Federal Desegregation Bill resulted in the complete integration of the military. Until that time, Blacks served in all-Black units, typically led by White officers. This was best depicted in the movie "Glory." Similar to Black men not being permitted to lead White men, Black women who were nurses could only treat the German Nazi prisoners of war.

Interestingly, while teaching at West Point, I learned about one of the most hateful systemic acts of anti-Black racism. Henry Ossian Flipper, a former enslaved man, was the first Black to graduate from West Point in 1877 and became the first Black person to lead the 10th Calvary's buffalo soldiers.[33] Prior to his appointment, all Black regiments were led by White officers. Aside from the inhumane experiences of slavery, Henry Ossian Flipper experienced further inhumanity at West Point. During his four years there, as the only Black cadet, he was silenced; that is, no other cadet spoke a word to him. Today, there is a bust of Henry Ossian Flipper on the campus of West Point and every year an award is given in his name to the cadet who exhibits "leadership, self-discipline, and perseverance in the face of unusual difficulties."[34]

A young Black man who is a music award winner and has never been silenced on a university campus is Kasseem Dean, also known as Swizz Beatz. I met him in the fall of 2015, when the president of HBS's African-American Student Union (AASU) came to my office and informed me that Swizz Beatz was on campus. I responded, "Who is that?" She told me he was a musical performer, producer, and Grammy Award winner. I asked if she wanted me to invite him to speak at the upcoming AASU Conference.

After she approved, I reached out to him in the HBS Executive Program that he was attending. We met and became immediate friends. He agreed to be a keynote speaker at the conference five months later. A few months later, he called to tell me he was being suspended from attending the second and third year of the HBS program where he was enrolled. His suspension was initiated by a professor who was entangled in a lawsuit brought on by someone who was a colleague of Kasseem's. Kasseem did nothing wrong! The professor was so angry that he got Kasseem expelled. I thought the entire action was unwarranted and unfair, so I agreed to help Kasseem. Over a four-week period, I had discussions with the professor, the director of the program, and two associate deans. Getting nowhere, I finally reached out to the dean with an email stating Kasseem's innocence and the fact that the world did not need to hear a story about a young Black man being expelled. I told the dean that Kasseem was the perfect example of our mission to "educate leaders who make a difference." My argument included the fact that he was a young Black male with millions of young Black male followers and by being at HBS he was showing them that education was cool. After a few more weeks of negotiating, a settlement was reached allowing Kasseem to complete the program. He did so in 2017 with his wife, Alicia Keys, beaming with pride in the audience at graduation.

My work helping the Black community of Englewood in Chicago is now in its tenth year. In 2011, a Fortune 500 company, Norfolk Southern Railroad Company, began buying homes in this poverty-stricken Black community. They even held a community meeting with armed guards, where they announced to the audience of homeowners that they wanted to purchase their homes for the expansion of Norfolk's freight yard. They told the attendees that they would buy their homes at fair market values of $20,000 to $80,000 and, if they did not sell voluntarily, they would take legal action to take the homes via eminent domain. This was the community of my childhood and where I still own the home purchased by my grandparents in 1952, when they were the first Black family on the block. Their mortgage was issued by the famous department store Sears, Roebuck and Co.

Many of the homeowners were like me. Their families had owned the homes for multiple generations, they were not ready to sell, or, if they were amenable, not for the prices offered. In response to Norfolk Southern's high-handed assault, we created an organization of 39 homeowners called the Englewood Railway Coalition. I was elected president of the new nonprofit organization, and we organized because we felt that Norfolk Southern was bullying a community of poor working-class Black citizens. There was a lot of news coverage, including an article in the *Chicago Tribune* titled "In Englewood, Railroad Presses on with Freight Yard Project."[35]

After the article was published, several articles followed in other newspapers. Additionally, there were a number of interviews and stories on television and radio newscasts. Many of my White business colleagues and friends saw the articles and news stories and queried me as to why I was involved in helping poor Black people fight a Fortune 500 company. At a board meeting, one asked, "Steve, why are you fighting against a business? You are a business school professor who believes in capitalism." I agreed with everything that he said and added, "I am a race man, always interested in helping the Black community. I believe in capitalism but not the 'Low Road' capitalism that has the objective of growing at all costs and abusing the powerless." This was the kind of capitalism used to enslave Black people from 1619 to 1865, and I saw remnants of it being practiced by Norfolk Southern.

Over the last ten years, 35 of the original 39 members of the coalition have settled with Norfolk Southern Railroad for prices that ranged from $120,000 to $538,000. Everyone received 200–400% more than was originally offered. The original offers would have left people in a state of constant poverty. For example, the woman offered $20,000 for her home could never have afforded to buy a new home. She would have been homeless within a year.

As people begin accepting settlements, I was concerned that they were doing so because my leadership was becoming less effective. I discussed this concern with a close friend, Ralph Moore, who owns his own consulting firm and is an expert in corporate diversity. Ralph told me, in the most beautifully supportive way, that I was looking at things completely wrong. He said the other members had to settle because it was as far as they could go. Their settlement for multiples greater than the original offers was a wonderful story of success.

Then he paralleled it to the history of Black people leaving the South after being enslaved, heading to the North. That Black migration, also known as the great Northward Migration, saw six million Black people exit southern states. Chicago was the ultimate destination for Blacks in Louisiana and Mississippi. Blacks from Texas went west to California, and those in Florida and North Carolina went to New York.

As Ralph explained, when Black people left Louisiana and Mississippi, they told the train ticket takers they were going to Chicago, but if they did not have enough money to take them all the way to Chicago they would say, "Give me a ticket to go as close as my money will let me to Chicago. I gotta get the heck out of the deep South."

The result was that Blacks exited the trains in cities between Mississippi and Chicago. Those cities included St. Louis, Kansas City, Des Moines, Springfield, and Indianapolis. While they did not reach their ideal destination of Chicago, the measure of their success was successfully exiting Mississippi. And that is the best measure of what the coalition accomplished. Everyone may not have reached their ideal settlement number, but all of them reached settlements that positively changed their lives, and the lives of future generations. I get tremendous joy and satisfaction from this success of contributing to wealth creation for 35 Black families. Even the eminent domain lawsuit against me by Norfolk Southern Railroad Co. (Figure 1.1) does not dampen that joy!

2017 IL App (1st) 162280-U

No. 1-16-2280

May 2, 2017

SECOND DIVISION

NOTICE: This order was filed under Supreme Court Rule 23 and may not be cited as precedent by any party except in the limited circumstances allowed under Rule 23(e)(1).

IN THE

APPELLATE COURT OF ILLINOIS

FIRST DISTRICT

NORFOLK SOUTHERN RAILWAY COMPANY,	))))	Appeal from the Circuit Court Of Cook County.
Plaintiff-Appellee,	))	
v.	)))	No. 16 L 050023 16 L 050024 16 L 0500131
STEVEN ROGERS, FNA ELM LLC, and UNKNOWN OWNERS,	)))	The Honorable Kay M. Hanlon,
Defendants-Appellees,	))	Judge Presiding.
MARGARET BONNETT, EARL MARVIN DENNIS, WILLIAM GRIFFIN, JP MORGAN CHASE BANK NA, and UNKNOWN OWNERS,	)))))	
Defendants-Appellees,	))	
v.	))	
ARC LAW GROUP, LLLP,	))	
Intervening Party-Appellant.	)	

JUSTICE NEVILLE delivered the judgment of the court.
Presiding Justice Hyman and Justice Mason concurred in the judgment.

Figure 1.1   Norfolk Southern Ry. Co. v. Rogers, 2017

When I taught my course titled "Entrepreneurial Finance for Black Entrepreneurs," I continually told my students that their ability as future entrepreneurs to raise money from investors would be largely based on trust. During her due diligence, the investor is trying to discern if she can trust the entrepreneur to do what he said he would do with building a business. I then told them that trust comes from one of two sources: blind faith or experience. Hopefully, this chapter has convinced you that you can trust me and my advice to you, because of my experiences with living in, investing in, studying, researching, and leading the Black community.

Notes

1. Fernandes, Deirdre. "At Harvard Business School, Diversity Remains Elusive." *Boston Globe.* June 1, 2019. https://www.bostonglobe.com/metro/2019/06/01/harvard-business-school-diversity-remains-elusive/bpyxP4cE1iCQJdLbHQEaQI/story.html
2. Byrne, John A. "Steven Rogers Letter to Harvard University President Larry Bacow." *Poets & Quants.* June 16, 2020. https://poetsandquants.com/2020/06/15/steven-rogers-letter-to-harvard-university-president-larry-bacow/?pq-category=business-school-news
3. Hendricks, Leta. "Research Guides: Africana Studies: Black Studies 2.0." (2015). https://guides.osu.edu/africana/raceman
4. Norwood, Arlisha. "Ida B. Wells-Barnett." National Women's History Museum. 2000. https://www.womenshistory.org/education-resources/biographies/ida-b-wells-barnett
5. Brown, DeNeen L. "Harriet Tubman Is Already Appearing on $20 Bills Whether Trump Officials Like It or Not." *Washington Post.* May 24, 2019. https://www.washingtonpost.com/history/2019/05/24/harriet-tubman-is-already-appearing-bills-whether-trump-officials-like-it-or-not/
6. Widmer, Ted. "Opinion: Why Two Black Athletes Raised Their Fists During the Anthem." *New York Times*, October 16, 2018. https://www.nytimes.com/2018/10/16/opinion/why-smith-and-carlos-raised-their-fists.html
7. Streeter, Kurt. "Kneeling, Fiercely Debated in the N.F.L., Resonates in Protests." *New York Times*, June 5, 2020. https://www.nytimes.com/2020/06/05/sports/football/george-floyd-kaepernick-kneeling-nfl-protests.html

8. "Did Muhammad Ali Throw His Gold Medal into the Ohio River?" n.d. www.Smithsonianchannel.com. https://www.smithsonianchannel.com/video/series/sports-detectives/49239

9. "Muhammad Ali Originally Named for Ardent Abolitionist and Yale Alumnus Cassius Clay." Yale News. June 9, 2016. https://news.yale.edu/2016/06/09/muhammad-ali-originally-named-ardent-abolitionist-and-yale-alumnus-cassius-clay

10. Iftekhar, Rubaid. "The Day Ali Threw Away His Olympic Gold into the Ohio River." *Business Standard*. April 17, 2020. https://tbsnews.net/sports/day-ali-threw-away-his-olympic-gold-ohio-river-70489

11. Orkand, Bob. "Opinion: 'I Ain't Got No Quarrel with Them Vietcong.'" *New York Times*. June 27, 2017. https://www.nytimes.com/2017/06/27/opinion/muhammad-ali-vietnam-war.html

12. Kubota, Samantha. "Tennis Star Naomi Osaka Joins Athlete Boycott in Protest of Jacob Blake Shooting." August 6, 2020. TODAY.com. https://www.today.com/popculture/tennis-star-naomi-osaka-boycotts-match-protest-jacob-blake-shooting-t190297

13. Ramsay, George. "These Were the Black Victims Naomi Osaka Honored on Face Masks at the US Open." CNN. September 14, 2020. https://edition.cnn.com/2020/09/11/tennis/naomi-osaka-us-open-face-mask-spt-intl/index.html

14. Kaur, Harmeet. "Magic Johnson Will Provide $100 Million to Fund Loans to Minority-Owned Businesses." CNN. May 19, 2020. https://www.cnn.com/2020/05/19/us/magic-johnson-capital-loans-minority-businesses-trnd/index.html

15. Green, Erica L. "Lebron James Opened a School That Was Considered an Experiment: It's Showing Promise." *New York Times*. April 12, 2019. https://www.nytimes.com/2019/04/12/education/lebron-james-school-ohio.html

16. "Juliette Hampton Morgan: A White Women Who Understood." Teaching Tolerance. Accessed January 14, 2021. https://www.tolerance.org/classroom-resources/tolerance-lessons/juliette-hampton-morgan-a-white-woman-who-understood

17. Ibid.

18. Anderson, Nick, and Lauren Lumpkin. "Transformational: MacKenzie Scott's Gifts to HBCUs, Other Colleges Surpass $800 Million." *Washington Post*. https://www.washingtonpost.com/local/education/mackenzie-scott-hbcu-donations/2020/12/17/0ce9ef5a-406f-11eb-8db8-395dedaaa036_story.html

19. Sheward, David. "The Real Story Behind 'Amazing Grace.'" *Biography*. March 17, 2016. https://www.biography.com/news/amazing-grace-story-john-newton

20. Grady, Denise. "H. Jack Geiger, Doctor Who Fought Social Ills, Dies at 95." *New York Times.* December 28, 2020. https://www.nytimes.com/2020/12/28/health/h-jack-geiger-dead.html

21. "'The Sit-In' Takes a Look at the Week Harry Belafonte Hosted the Tonight Show." n.d. MSNBC.com. https://www.msnbc.com/the-reidout/watch/-the-sit-in-takes-a-look-at-the-week-harry-belafonte-hosted-the-tonight-show-91371589559

22. "Martin Luther King Jr.: 'The Economic Problem Is the Most Serious Problem' – YouTube." n.d. www.Youtube.com. https://www.youtube.com/watch?v=fmauhsmcY2c.

23. Coleman, Colette. "How the 1968 Sanitation Workers' Strike Expanded the Civil Rights Struggle." HISTORY.com. July 21, 2020. https://www.history.com/news/sanitation-workers-strike-memphis

24. Adams, Lucy. "MLK's Last Words 'Play Precious Lord." *The Mountaineer.* April 11, 2018. https://www.themountaineer.com/life/religion/mlks-last-words-play-precious-lord/article_92643c7a-379a-11e8-a838-bbdc19724829.html#:~:text=King%20said%2C%20%22Ben%2C%20play

25. "Mahalia Jackson Sings April 1968 Martin Luther King Funeral - TV Footage (Live) (Spirituals Songs) – YouTube." n.d. www.Youtube.com. https://www.youtube.com/watch?v=ohT76YI0hT0

26. "Talented Tenth | Educational Concept." 2019. In *Encyclopedia Britannica.* https://www.britannica.com/topic/Talented-Tenth

27. "What Is an HBCU?" HBCU Lifestyle. Accessed December 27, 2020. https://hbculifestyle.com/what-is-an hbcu/#:~:text=HBCU%20Meaning&text=%E2%80%9Cany%20historically%20Black%20college%20or,by%20the%20Secretary%20of%20Education.%E2%80%9D

28. Kirshenbaum, Jerry. "On the Wrong Course." *Sports Illustrated.* July 4, 1983. https://vault.si.com/vault/1983/07/04/scorecard

29. "Segregated Club Out as Golf Host." *New York Times.* July 15, 1983. https://www.nytimes.com/1983/07/15/sports/segregated-club-out-as-golf-host.html

30. Flood, Gay. "19th Hole: The Readers Take Over." *Sports Illustrated.* August 1, 1983. https://vault.si.com/vault/1983/08/01/19th-hole-the-readers-take-over

31. "Ariel Education Initiative." n.d. Ariel Education Initiative. Accessed December 27, 2020. https://www.arieleducationinitiative.org/

32. Kagan, Sam. "PRINCO Claims It Prioritizes Diversity. Experts Want Proof." *Princetonian.* May 2, 2020. https://www.dailyprincetonian.com/article/2020/05/princeton-endowment-princo-diversity-sharpton

33. "Second Lieutenant Henry O. Flipper: First Black Graduate of West Point." Fort David National Historic Site. n.d. https://www.buffalosoldier.net/HenryO.Flipper2.htm

34. "Henry O. Flipper: Overcoming Adversity Through Perseverance." Thayer Leadership. February 10, 2017. https://www.thayerleadership.com/blog/2017/ henry-o.-flipper-overcoming-adversity-through-perseverance#:~:text= Flipper%2C%20the%20first%20African%2DAmerican,in%20the%20 face%20of%20adversity

35. Bowean, Lolly. "In Englewood, Railroad Presses on with Freight Yard Project." *Chicago Tribune*. March 2, 2016. https://www.chicagotribune.com/ news/ct-englewood-railroad-grows-met-0303-20160302-story.html

CHAPTER TWO

How the Wealth Gap
Was Created

White Americans' hold on wealth is old, deep, and nearly unshakable. . . . Crucial to understanding how to close that gap – such that it can actually be closed – is grappling with how it was created in the first place.[1]

IT IS MY belief that most Whites know that the Black community is poor, but do not know the depth of that poverty nor the reasons why. One of the reasons behind this absence of knowledge is the failure of Whites to learn the complete history of our country. Specifically, what was missing from their education was a deeper learning of the history of Black Americans. Whether through acts of commission or omission (or both), our primary, secondary, and collegiate educational systems excluded teaching about the root causes of how the Black community came to be where it is today. Since that history was not a standard part of the pedagogy in academia, it was never taught in the classroom.

That is the reason why only 8% of high school seniors know that slavery was one of the main reasons for the Civil War.[2]

In fact, according to one study, 75% of White Americans have no nonwhite friends.[3] Conversely, for those Whites who do have Black friends, the relationship can be quite frustrating for the latter when it comes to discussing issues of Blackness. For example, when Nikole Hannah-Jones, the Pulitzer Prize–winning writer for the *New York Times*, was asked about her discussions with White friends about Black issues, she said that those discussions are usually challenging because most White people know so little about Black life and history. Accordingly, she must often begin the conversation with a brief Black history lesson.[4]

The absence of inclusion and information about Blacks is not limited to our history books. In my own experience as a professor at Harvard Business School, I noticed the general exclusion of Black achievements in the course curricula. The *Washington Post* reported my dissatisfaction with this fact in a 2017 article with a headline that read, "Only 2 of the 300 Case Studies Read by First-Year Harvard Business School Students Include Black Executives."[5] The result of this omission of Black accomplishments at Harvard Business School propelled me to create a new course, "Black Business Leaders and Entrepreneurship." I wrote 24 case studies with Black business protagonists, specifically excluding athletes and entertainers. The interest in a course featuring Black people was so widespread that students from 9 of Harvard's 14 schools enrolled. They came from the schools of Business, Law, Engineering, Medical, Design, Education, Public Policy, Divinity, and the undergraduate college. Students also cross-registered from M.I.T. The course was taught to over 130 students; only three were White. Tellingly, White students avoided the opportunity to learn something about Black achievements in business and, for them, just as in our history books, Blacks were omitted.

One of the most disappointing conversations that I have ever had about the role of race was with a White person concerning the viewpoints of many White economists. This conversation touched on the fact that well-educated White people minimized the importance of the enslavement of Black people in the wealth creation for Whites involved in cotton farming. While I was teaching at Harvard Business School, a new professor from Harvard College moved into the office next to mine. His name was Sven Beckert. When I visited his office to introduce myself, I noticed a book on his desk titled *Empire of Cotton: A Global History*. I picked the book up and noted that he was the author. I remarked that the book must at least be 50% about the enslavement of Black people and their importance to the prosperity of the cotton industry. He said that my assumption was right, but that I would probably be surprised to learn that my assumption was not common. He then went on to tell me that when he presented his book and its theses to fellow academics at conferences, it was not unusual to have critics who opined that he was giving too much credit to the use of free Black labor as one of the main factors contributing to the wealth creation of the cotton industry. Those who said he exaggerated the significance of Blacks argued that the cotton producers would have simply replaced enslaved unpaid Blacks with cheap paid labor by other races.

This Pollyannish argument defies the fundamentals of basic finance, which says that the popularity of a product is enhanced when it can be sold cheaply. Before the Civil War, the U.S. sold and produced 75% of the cotton in the world.[6] Many other countries, including India and Egypt, also produced cotton, but their financial success was lower because they could not produce cotton at a cost lower than America's. Labor costs for the average business has consistently been 30 to 50% of the product's selling price. The White-owned cotton plantations in America had direct labor costs of $0.00 on their income statements. The absence of this expense created enormous profits such that by the dawn of the Civil War, the Mississippi River Valley, home to thousands of cotton plantations, had more millionaires per capita than any other region in the country.[7]

By 1850, the cotton industry used the free labor of around 1.8 million Black enslaved people to clear the land, plant the seeds, pick the cotton, and clean it to be sold.[8] Cotton produced by Black enslaved people in America accounted for 77% of the 800 million pounds of cotton used in Britain; 90% of the 192 million pounds used in France; 60% of the 115 million pounds used in the Zollverein; and 92% of the 102 million pounds used in Russia. As one British bureaucrat commented, this dominance is "owing to the toil and suffering of the Negro."[9]

In 2020, following the George Floyd murder, Whites began reversing their incomplete knowledge of Blacks. Books about Black people or subjects related to Blacks sold in record numbers, and sales of top books about race increased by up to 6,800%.[10] As one Black person said about her White friends, "They promise to 'educate themselves' about race in America."[11] It is in this spirit of such self-education that I write this chapter as a summary of the rudimentary causes of the Black-White wealth gap in our country. Without this knowledge, I believe that my request of you in the subsequent chapters will not have the same impact. My hope for my challenge to you and its desired effect is for you to personally take action towards righting a wrong done to Black Americans. What was done to Blacks, primarily facilitated by or through the agency of the federal and local governments, was done to benefit Whites financially at the expense Blacks. Those things included vagrancy laws, Black Codes, Jim Crow laws, anti-Black deeds and covenants, redlining, and slavery.

The Roots of Black American Poverty

The forced enslavement of Black people, approved and sanctioned by the British government and later by the U.S. federal government, has been called the greatest crime ever against humanity, as well as America's first big business.[12] The financial commerce aspect and benefits of this system were the primary reason why our government approved, supported, and encouraged the bondage of Black people. It was not a few "bad apple pirates" who committed this barbaric crime. It was the government itself that allowed over 12 million Africans to be forcibly transported almost 9,000 miles from the continent of Africa to the Americas; this was the transatlantic slave trade.[13] This movement of human cargo—to what is now the U.S. by British-government sanctioned companies, lasted 157 years, from 1619 to 1776. British North America's inaugural settlement was in Virginia, where the first 20 enslaved Africans were taken. The first documented legal statement forcing Blacks into lifetime servitude was in 1640 when John Punch, a Black man, was ordered by the courts to "serve his said master or his assigns for the time of his natural life here or elsewhere."[14] This was the first of thousands of such legal decisions, public policies, and laws issued over 24 decades that had the specific, clear, and biased objective of financially benefiting Whites at the inhuman expense of Blacks. Permitting Whites to have this free labor was nothing short of a government subsidy or handout to Whites for 246 years.

Other laws enacted during the reign of the British in North America are shown in the following timeline:[15]

- 1662: Law decrees that the children of Black enslaved women shall inherit their mother's slave status even if the father is a free White man.

- 1667: Law states that baptizing an enslaved Black person does not free them from bondage.
- 1672: The King of England encourages the Royal African Company to import more Black slaves.
- 1698: The government licenses companies other than the Royal African Company to import Black slaves. This new law results in an increase of Africans transported to British North American colonies from 5,000 to 45,000 per year.
- 1705: The government defines slaves as people who are not Christians in their native country. The law additionally states, "All Negro, mulatto and Indian slaves within this dominion . . . shall be held to be real estate. If any slave resist his master . . . correcting such slave, and shall happen to be killed in such correction . . . the master shall be free of all punishment . . . as if such accident never happened."

While killing one's own slave was not a punishable act for Whites, many preferred not to kill their slaves because they were the means by which they gained wealth and by which their wealth was measured.

One particularly barbaric punishment of a Black slave was described in the diaries of Thomas Thistlewood, a slave plantation overseer. He described the following punishment of an enslaved man in his diary for July 1756: "Gave him a moderate whipping, pickled him well, and made Hector shit in his mouth, immediately put in a gag whilst his mouth was full & made him wear it 4 to 5 hours."[16] The arbitrary nature of this punishment reinforced the absolute power White masters wielded over their property, Black slaves.

Further exploration of the range of punishments for Black slaves reveals that there were also laws that specifically identified the punishment to be given for specific violations, such as the 1642 Virginia Fugitive Law, which authorized branding of runaway slaves by applying a hot iron to the face.[17] If a slave was found guilty of murder, he was to be hanged immediately. For robbery, the enslaved Black person would receive 60 lashes and have his or her ear cut off. For minor violations, such as associating with Whites, slaves were whipped, branded, or maimed.[18] Black enslaved people fought back many times by poisoning White owners. A law was enacted to address this issue in 1748, a few years after Eve, an enslaved Black, was found guilty of poisoning her owner. Her punishment was execution by public burning.[19]

All of this human carnage was a part of an industry with the singular objective of creating wealth for Whites. And it worked. Even the freedom that Americans gained from the Revolutionary War was not extended to enslaved Blacks. They remained the primary source of free labor for the sole purpose of enriching Whites. As one slave owner stated, "The principal product that will elevate us from poverty is cotton, and we cannot do this without the help of slaves."[20]

Despite philosophical ideals concerning personal freedom and national identity based on the will of the people, the most prominent legal document allowing continued enslavement of Black people was the U.S. Constitution. The Constitution was ratified in 1787 by 55 delegates, 49% (27) of whom were slave-owning White men, including George Washington and James Madison, future presidents of the United States. The major flaw in the U.S. Constitution was its intentional mistreatment of Blacks relative to and for the benefit of Whites. This is the reason that many legal scholars, including Professor Juan Perea from Loyola University School of Law, has referred to the Constitution as the "proslavery Constitution."[21] For example, the Constitution permitted the counting of an enslaved person as three-fifths of a person. This clause was included so that states with large slave populations could count 60% of that population as American citizens, specifically for the purpose of political representation in Congress. This government representation assured slave owners that they could continue to make money without the constant threat of the abolition of slavery.

The government support of slavery was not solely through instruments like the Constitution, but also through state laws that rewarded slave owners. The states of South Carolina and Texas passed laws designed to incentivize slave owners to move to their states. Those states gave free land to White plantation owners who moved to their states and brought enslaved Black people with them. In the late 1800s, the government of Texas enacted public finance subsidy laws providing new settlers with 80 acres of free land for each enslaved person they brought to the state with them. Like the U.S. Constitution, the Texas Constitution supported slavery. Section 9 of the Texas Constitution read, "nor shall congress have the power to emancipate slaves; nor shall any slave holder be allowed to emancipate his or her slave without the consent of congress, unless he or she shall send his or her slave or slaves without the limits of the republic."[22]

The importance of slavery to states like Texas was clear from the language of their constitutions. The specific importance of slavery lies in its role in the wealth creation of a White family. Felicia Furman explains the importance of slavery when she discusses the journey of her forebears, who moved from New York to Charleston, South Carolina, to take advantage of the free land being offered. Their slaves worked the land that brought wealth to the family for multiple generations. After learning the truth of her family's slavery-based wealth, Furman said, "I became horrified that slavery was such a big part of who we are as Americans, that enslaving people enriched so many families, including mine." She went on to say, "There is no act that can atone for what my family did to their families."[23] Furman has made a documentary, titled *Shared History*,[24] about her family and the Black families who are descendants of people enslaved by the Furmans. From the documentary we learn that one of her slave-owning relatives founded Furman University. She also reveals that another relative, Reverend James C. Furman, was a Baptist minister and college professor, teaching a course on the philosophy of religion. One day, this man of God dismissed his students early so that they could go to Greenville, South Carolina, to attend the public lynching of a Black person. Reverend Furman was a strong supporter of the Confederacy, which was not subtle about the importance of enslaving Black people for financial enrichment. The industry of slavery was so important that the states that seceded and created the Confederacy also created their own currency. Most of this currency included depictions of Black enslaved men and women engaged in physical labor, such as hoeing fields to plant cotton, picking cotton, and transporting bales of cotton on cattle-drawn wagons.[25]

This story of slavery, White wealth, and Black poverty was best described in 2020 by a Black woman named Kimberly Jones, a young writer and activist. In a video with over three-quarters of a million views, she described eloquently, with a high degree of pain and frustration, the economic cancer that slavery inflicted on Black Americans. Using a popular board game, she analogized that slavery for Black people was like playing Monopoly against White people, where for 246 years, when Black people went around the board, we had to give away 100% of our winnings to our White opponents. Explicitly, we never got to keep a penny for almost 12 generations. As a consequence, unlike our fellow White countrymen, most Black Americans have never experienced the wonder of intergenerational wealth transfer compounding those long years of denial, and then, even after slavery ended, the attacks by Whites against the financial well-being of Blacks continued.[26]

White slaveholders and non-White slaveholders benefited from the one-sided winner in the "Monopoly game" of slavery. Many publicly owned blue chip Fortune 500 companies had a relationship with slavery, from their inception or predecessors' entities. The industries included railroads, investment banks, commercial banks, media, jewelry, and clothing.[27] For example, Brooks Brothers, a high-end clothing company, sold clothes for enslaved people. Tiffany and Co., a high-end jeweler, received its initial funding from a company directly involved in slavery. Insurance companies, including New York Life, Aetna, and American International Group (AIG), wrote policies that paid slave owners if enslaved people died. The predecessors of banks, including JP Morgan Chase, Wells Fargo, Bank of America, and Citibank, provided loans to slave owners and often took their enslaved people as collateral. In fact, Chase's predecessor accepted 13,000 enslaved people as collateral.

Whites have reaped enormous wealth benefits from generations of their participation in the Black slave industry. Even the symbol of U.S. capitalism, Wall Street, was a beneficiary of, and stood in the reflection of, the Black slave institution. The largest slave market where Black children, men, and women were sold stood a mere two blocks from the New York Stock Exchange.[28]

The End of Bondage

For about 160 years, Black Americans across the country have attended Watch Night services at churches on New Year's Eve, beginning on December 31, 1862.[29] This tradition is in recognition of Black enslaved people being freed from the institution that did not pay them for their work, while creating wealth for twelve generations of Whites. Some refer to that first Watch Night as "Freedom's Eve" because it was the night before the Emancipation Proclamation came into effect, liberating four million enslaved people. On that night, Blacks gathered in churches awaiting the news that the law was enacted, granting them freedom.

Despite the Proclamation, many White slaveholders refused to inform their enslaved people that they were no longer the legal property of another human being. To do so would wreck their business model that relied on zero costs for direct labor. There-fore, many slave owners moved their operations to Texas, where the word of emancipation did not reach Black people until June 19, 1865. On that day, Major General Gordon Granger arrived in Galveston, Texas, and ordered the immediate emancipation of all enslaved people.[30] As a consequence, this date is celebrated annually by Black Americans as Juneteenth.

Black Codes

Even after slavery ended in 1865, federal and local laws con-tinued for the purpose of benefiting Whites at the expense of Blacks. Just as with slavery, these laws enabled the wealth gen-eration of Whites by facilitating that Blacks work for minimal or effectively no compensation. Accordingly, these laws had the impact of financially rewarding Whites at a cost to Blacks.

The Southern states, which had been part of the Confederacy that lost the Civil War, had the freedom to enact self-serving laws. The federal government never tried former Confederate soldiers for treason, and they were allowed to keep their land. The only obligations former Confederate soldiers had to fulfill was to swear loyalty to the Union, pay off their war debt, and agree to support the Constitution's 13th Amendment, which had abolished slavery.

With no federal laws specifically restricting the abuse and exploitation of the former enslaved people, now called freedmen, local governments created a new system that continued the wealth gap between Blacks and Whites. This system, which Pulitzer Prize winner Douglas A. Blackmon described as slavery by another name, was governed by the Black Codes. Each state created their own Black Codes, but all of them had the same objective of financially helping Whites while hurting Blacks. In a perverse case of unintended consequences, the 13th Amendment freed Blacks from one form of bondage into another. While slavery was abolished, the amendment gave birth to Black Codes that contained the provision that enslavement is a legal punishment for crime.[31]

The Black Codes in Southern states included the requirement that every Black person in the state must have a labor contract.[32] This contract was a written document, signed by a judge, indicating that the "servant," the Black freedman, had an obligation to work for a specific White "master." Simply stated, these labor contracts sanctioned a form of legal duress, with the threat of punishment from the government. The first such contract requirement was enacted in Mississippi's Black Codes, passed by the government on November 22, 1865, a little more than six months following the end of the Civil War.

The final sentence of such contracts often resulted in the Black person owing the "employer" the money (i.e., the actual wages) that he had been paid. If this "debt" could not be paid the "employee" was jailed for default on a "loan."

All contracts for labor made with freedmen, free negroes and mulattoes for a longer period than one month shall be in writing, and a duplicate, attested and read to said freedman, free negro or mulatto by a beat, city or county officer . . . and if the laborer shall quit the service of the employer before the expiration of his term of service, without good cause, he shall forfeit his wages for that year up to the time of quitting.[33]

A typical legal sentence was forced labor, where the arresting authorities were paid by private businesses, such as railroad companies, for the labor services of the "employee." This was called convict leasing. Plantation owners or others who wanted additional labor went to the courthouse to purchase imprisoned Blacks. A Black person could end up in this unpaid working condition for any number of reasons. An arrest of a Black person could be made arbitrarily by a government official or by any White citizen, for any reason. The following is an example of the law as it pertained to the employment of a Black person:

> Every civil officer shall, and every person may, arrest and carry back to his or her legal employer any freedman, free negro, or mulatto who shall have quit the service of his or her employer before the expiration of his or her term of service without good cause.[34]

In addition to Blacks being fed into the convict leasing system via labor contracts, it was also common for them to be found guilty of vagrancy laws, which were part of the Black Codes. Black men and women were arrested and guilty of vagrancies violations for not having jobs, for being unable to show documents proving that they were employed, or for "having jobs that did not serve the interest of whites."[35] As noted in Mississippi's Vagrancy Law, almost anybody could be found guilty, and Black people were.[36]

> That all rogues and vagabonds, idle and dissipated persons, beggars, jugglers, or persons practicing unlawful games or plays, runaways, common drunkards, common night-walkers,

pilferers, lewd, wanton, or lascivious persons, in speech or
behavior, common railers and brawlers, persons who neglect
their calling or employment, misspend what they earn, or do
not provide for the support of themselves or their families, or
dependents, and all other idle and disorderly persons, including all who neglect all lawful business, habitually misspend
their time by frequenting houses of ill-fame, gaming-houses, or
tippling shops, shall be deemed and considered vagrants, under
the provisions of this act, and upon conviction thereof shall
be fined not exceeding one hundred dollars, with all accruing
costs, and be imprisoned, at the discretion of the court, not
exceeding ten days.

Like their predecessor, slavery, vagrancy laws exploited Black
adults and their children. If a person was found guilty of being
"vagrant," the courts were authorized to apprentice his or her
children, even against their will, to an employer until the age of
21 for males and 18 for females.[37] All of these Black Codes had the
ultimate effect of wealth creation for Whites and a life of poverty
for Blacks. According to the commanding general in Virginia,
Alfred H. Terry, the White employers were conspiring to pay
people wages "below the real value of their labor," and "wages
utterly inadequate to the support of themselves and families."[38]
These Black Codes were intent to stop Blacks from accumulating
wealth and generating assets, including land and homes.

Home Ownership and Wealth Creation

As Robert Johnson, the founder of Black Entertainment Television, stated, if you are going to accumulate wealth, the most
important asset you can have is a home.[39] Johnson was not the
first to believe that home ownership is an essential component of
wealth creation. The United States federal government believed

it also and implemented a plan that resulted in wealth creation for the White community. The instrument of White wealth generation that the government used was White-owned banks.

After World War II, there was a housing boom in America, fueled by the Federal Housing Administration (FHA), which was part of the New Deal. At the time the country had a miniscule middle class. Citizens were either poor or rich. Suburbia did not exist. Most home mortgages were amortized over five years with a balloon payment at the end. For the mortgages that existed during the Depression, almost half were in default. The foreclosure rate was almost 1,000 per day. People primarily lived in cities, but, most significantly, prior to 1934, 20- and 30-year home mortgages did not exist. Therefore, only the wealthy could afford to own homes.

This dynamic changed for White citizens with the creation of the FHA, which allowed mortgages to be refinanced and guaranteed for new buyers. Banks could issue mortgages because the federal government was assuming the risk. The results were that White banks issued millions of loans to White citizens, helping them create wealth. However, access to this capital was not available to Black Americans. In fact, the federal government forbade it.

The population that benefitted from this discriminatory housing policy was White: 98% of the private mortgages the FHA issued between 1930 and 1950 were received by White Americans, and only 2% receiving FHA loans were non-White.[40] This anti-Black government policy is known to us as redlining. Property deed covenants reflected this discriminatory practice through restrictive contract language such as "land or buildings thereon shall never be rented, leased or sold, transferred or conveyed to, nor shall same be occupied exclusively by person or persons other than of the Caucasian Race," which was legal and enforceable.[41] And this practice of redlining was not limited to the South.

In Seattle, Washington, a deed read, "No person other than one of the White race shall ever be permitted to occupy any portion of any building, except as a domestic servant."[42]

If you wonder how and why Black and White neighborhoods differ the way they do, the following is a clear roadmap of how this evolved. First, those living in or near Black communities were intentionally and callously denied capital. The economic impact, and the harm it caused, was real, quantifiable, and long lasting. In 1948, the Supreme Court case of *Shelley v. Kraemer* terminated the use of racially restrictive covenants since the enforcement of such covenants violated the 14th Amendment. Redlining was deemed illegal in 1968. Yet today, a lingering impact of redlining is reflected in the fact that only 44% of Blacks own their home, versus 72% of Whites. Black home ownership is the lowest of any racial or ethnic group in the country. An ironic bit of trivia is that the city with the greatest difference in homeownership rates (78% for Whites compared to 25% for Blacks) is Minneapolis, where George Floyd was murdered.[43]

Home Owners' Loan Corporation (HOLC)

As part of the New Deal in 1933, the federal government created the Home Owners' Loan Corporation (HOLC). In partnership with the FHA, this organization, in the words of Jacob William Faber, "boosted racial residential segregation and contributed to the racial wealth gap in the U.S."[44] The HOLC's role in the U.S. housing market was to act as an igniter through innovative programs and tools like the amortized mortgage (with 20- to 30-year terms) replacing the 5-year mortgage that carried large balloon payments at the end of the contract. The programs also purchased and refinanced existing mortgages that were at risk of default. HOLC initiated Residential Security Maps, a market intelligence tool that was used to gather information on neighborhood demographics.[45] People, including realtors, appraisers, and developers who were familiar with the local market, completed standardized surveys that were then analyzed by HOLC. The neighborhoods received letter grades, from A to D, and assigned a corresponding color code. Areas given an A grade were colored green and considered to be highly valuable. Conversely, the highest-risk neighborhoods (high crime, low income, and/or Black residents) were given a D grade and the color red, thus creating the term "redlined." With a letter grade and color, the life trajectory of millions of Black families was undercut, deflated, and derailed at a time of unparalleled growth for America generally. I make this observation because if you received a D and were assigned the color red, HOLC would not secure loans and, subsequently, banks would refuse to loan money to those living or looking to operate a business in or near redlined areas.

I live in Evanston, Illinois, a suburb of Chicago with a 16% Black population. I love it so much that I call it "Heavenston!" This beautiful community is also home to Northwestern University. It is also a community that has experienced the anti-Black racism of the HOLC. A report written by the federal government organization stated, "This concentration of negros in Evanston is quite a serious problem for the town as they seem to be growing steadily and encroaching into adjoining neighborhoods. The neighborhood is graded 'D' because of its concentration of negros, but the section may improve as this element is forced out."[46] This action by the federal government directly hindered the wealth creation opportunities of Black Evanstonians. The city of Evanston is trying to right this wrong with the creation of a reparations program.

I reviewed HOLC surveys via the Mapping Inequality Project from the University of Richmond, Virginia.[47] Launched in 2016, it is an interactive tool that allows you to see surveys and maps throughout the U.S. A cursory look at the one for Richmond and the template looked somewhat benign. It had the name of the city, the terrain type, and the building or construction types. However, on further inspection, a most horrific element of the document was reflected in its reference to the demographics on the map. Inhabitants were specifically listed as a line item (for instance, one line read "Negro %"). Those who requested these maps also wanted them to illustrate/detail information pertinent to city planning, such as the location and the percentage of foreign-born residents or "relief" families (people receiving government aid). At the end of the first page of the document, there is an area for clarifying remarks. The assessor for this document stated, "Respectable people but homes are too near negro area D2." The assessor gave the city of Richmond a security grade of C.

Let us pause for a moment and consider this point: the assessor downgraded the value of a neighborhood because of its proximity to a Black community. Actually, that Richmond community will get mistreated and will probably end up incurring a higher cost of living as a consequence of greater difficulty obtaining loans or an unfavorable borrowing rate, thus creating an environment of resentment and misunderstanding. Furthermore, the Black people living in "Area D2" are trapped in their district because of the limited resources available to them. Banks can only lend if they are willing to assume all of the risk. And, finally, Black people typically held property deeds with restrictive covenants containing racist language that was legally enforceable until 1948. Again, if you ever wonder how and why Black and White neighborhoods look the way they do, these elements present a clear explanation. Black people were intentionally and callously denied access to capital, even when they were not attempting to buy a house in a White neighborhood.

As columnist Natalie Moore reported recently, the real estate explosion was something akin to the 1946 movie *It's a Wonderful Life*. The movie's protagonist, George Bailey, was like our government and the FHA, helping people buy homes and live happier lives, but only for Whites. Black Americans were less fortunate, and their parallel part in this movie was a lot bleaker. In their lives, the government and the FHA operated much like the twisted, greedy, callous antagonist, Mr. Potter.[48]

This federally mandated policy created an American apartheid when it provided a generational wealth springboard for White families, while simultaneously denying Black people equitable access to a similar springboard. Black people were denied the loans necessary to purchase homes or start businesses in their own communities because the FHA and HOLC did not extend guarantees to loans in "D" redlined areas. The New Deal did not include Black people, who were almost exclusively left out of one of the greatest wealth creation periods in U.S. history. The New Deal created arguably the most prosperous decades in American history. The federal government partnered with the private sector and created millions of jobs in banking, real estate, and construction, while it helped millions of Americans keep their homes or buy new ones.

As the capital flowed to these newly created communities, now known as the suburbs, urban areas became more blighted and, instead of being springboards, they became graves where Black wealth went to die. Another example of how the government assisted White wealth creation was when the FHA established a program for home improvement loans that did not require collateral and was backed by the federal government.[49] With redlining becoming an unofficial but pervasive law of the land, Black communities continued to fall apart while the wealth of Whites continued to grow. Most significantly, as we look into the future of the baby boomer generation, of which I am a member, their descendants will be the direct beneficiaries of the wealth created via the New Deal. In fact, they are in a position to pass along a staggering $68 trillion in amassed fortunes to their children and charities over the next 25 years.[50] Sadly, very little of those fortunes will be transferred from one Black generation to the next because Black families have not been positioned to accumulate or pass it along. The *New York Times* recently reported that the average Black family passes along $38,000 to their heirs, compared to $140,000 for the average White family.[51] Research shows that the level of education is an irrelevant factor for this disparity. Even among college-educated families, only 13% of Blacks leave an inheritance of more than $10,000, compared to 41% for White families.[52]

Keeping Suburbs White

White real estate developers and homeowners in the new all-White suburbs also enjoyed the benefit of government largesse. A great example is Levittown, New York, the first suburb in America. The Levitt family built this community with construction loans from banks that were FHA guaranteed. The government required that the homes not be sold to Black citizens. More pointedly, the government mandated that each deed include a clause that prohibited the resale of the home to a Black American.[53]

A biting irony of discriminatory practices such as restrictive deeds is that Black veterans, such as Eugene Burnett, who had honorably served his country in the military, saw the newly established Long Island suburb as the perfect place to begin his postwar life, but were not allowed to purchase the homes. "It was as though it wasn't real," Burnett's wife, Bernice, recalled. "Look at this house! Can you imagine having this? And then for them to tell me because of the color of my skin that I can't be part of it?"[54] The Burnetts were just one of many Black families denied the opportunity for economic advancement through the purchase of a home. The Levittown story is significant because it was the first suburb built and marketed to returning World War II veterans in the years 1947 to 1951. Levittown was the beginning of a cultural shift that recognized the challenges of a world that would include men and women returning from the war effort and heading back to their traditional gender roles. Every finished home was equipped with televisions and modern kitchens.

The first 2,000 plots sold rapidly in 1947, and those sales continued until 1951, when they finished building Levittown and the surrounding area, which included over 17,000 Levitt-designed homes. A key element of this rapid growth was that these mass-produced homes were the product of standardized manufacturing processes operating at lower costs. Homes cost around $8,000 at the end of the 1940s, with the G.I. Bill reducing this cost to only $400 for qualifying veterans. The median price for a Levitt home in today's market is $400,000.[55]

On the other side of the country, in California, a cooperative of 400 families, which included novelist Wallace Stegner, wanted to duplicate the planned suburban phenomenon of Levittown. They purchased vacant land in close proximity to Stanford University for the purpose of building single-family homes. Amazingly, the FHA refused to guarantee the construction loan as it had for the Levitt family. The only reason was that 3 of the 400 families were Black Americans.[56] Learning that the rejection was based on race, the cooperative attempted to negotiate and proposed a compromise in which the percentage of Black ownership would never exceed the percentage of Black Americans in the state. Again, the FHA refused the guarantee. The land was eventually sold to another private developer who agreed to the total anti-Black restriction that the FHA demanded. As a consequence of including the anti-Black restriction, the developer was able to build hundreds of single-family homes with construction loans guaranteed by the FHA.[57]

The historic, systemic collusion practices between the government and the private sector have enslaved Blacks, subjected us to Black Codes, and denied us full participation in wealth creation through the acquisition of real estate, resulting in the Black community existing in a perpetual and chronic state of poverty. In contrast, those aforementioned actions have made the U.S. White community one of the wealthiest in the world. Those who supported slavery, the Black Codes, and redlining must view the huge Black-White wealth gap as confirmation that this "plan" was a huge success. Their desired objectives were achieved. The level of White wealth in America is virtually unattainable by Blacks. One study concluded that even if Whites acquired no additional wealth, it would take Black families over 225 years to amass the same degree of wealth as White families enjoy now.[58] It is no coincidence that those 225 years represent just a single generation less than the 246 years of slavery.

Notes

1. Mock, Brentin. "White Americans' Hold on Wealth Is Old, Deep, and Nearly Unshakeable." Bloomberg. September 3, 2019. https://www.bloomberg.com/news/articles/2019-09-03/the-amazing-resiliency-of-white-wealth
2. Walker, Tim. "U.S. Students' Disturbing Lack of Knowledge About Slavery." National Education Association. February 7, 2018. https://www.nea.org/advocating-for-change/new-from-nea/us-students-disturbing-lack-knowledge-about-slavery
3. Ghiglione, Loren. "Op-ed: What I Learned about White Privilege through 150 Interviews across America." *Chicago Tribune*. December 29, 2020. https://www.chicagotribune.com/opinion/commentary/ct-opinion-race-america-20201229-ljwibunpqjgwhj44ytd6to54sy-story.html

4. Gross, Terry. "A Call for Reparations: Nikole Hannah-Jones on the Wealth Gap." NPR. June 24, 2020. https://www.npr.org/2020/06/24/882927446/a-call-for-reparations-nikole-hannah-jones-on-the-wealth-gap

5. Jan, Tracy. "Only 2 of the 300 Case Studies Read by First-Year Harvard Business School Students Include Black Executives." *Washington Post.* April 14, 2017. https://www.washingtonpost.com/news/wonk/wp/2017/04/14/harvard-business-schools-first-year-curriculum-featured-300-business-leaders-only-2-were-black/

6. "History of Cotton." Pearce Museum. Accessed January 11, 2021. https://www.pearcemuseum.com/education/fifth-grade-curriculum/cotton-2/#:~:text=By%201860%2C%20Southern%20plantations%20supplied,and%20a%20few%20other%20ports.

7. Lockhart, P.R. "How Slavery Became America's First Big Business." Vox. August 16, 2019. https://www.vox.com/identities/2019/8/16/20806069/slavery-economy-capitalism-violence-cotton-edward-baptist

8. "The Economics of Cotton." Lumen Learning. Accessed January 11, 2021. https://courses.lumenlearning.com/ushistory1os/chapter/the-economics-of-cotton/

9. Beckert, Sven. "Empire of Cotton." *Atlantic.* December 12, 2014. https://www.theatlantic.com/business/archive/2014/12/empire-of-cotton/383660/

10. McEvoy, Jemima. "Sales of 'White Fragility' – And Other Anti-Racism Books – Jumped Over 2000% After Protests Began." *Forbes.* July 22, 2020. https://www.forbes.com/sites/jemimamcevoy/2020/07/22/sales-of-white-fragility-and-other-anti-racism-books-jumped-over-2000-after-protests-began/?sh=59a33c9e303d

11. Reid, Megan. "My White Friends Are Buying Books About Racism Instead of Talking to Me." Bustle. June 3, 2020. https://www.bustle.com/p/my-white-friends-are-buying-books-about-racism-i-wish-theyd-talked-to-me-instead-22954330

12. Lockhart, P.R. "How Slavery Became America's First Big Business." Vox. August 16, 2019. https://www.vox.com/identities/2019/8/16/20806069/slavery-economy-capitalism-violence-cotton-edward-baptist

13. Mintz, Steven. "Historical Context: Facts About the Slave Trade and Slavery." Gilder Lehrman Institute of American History. Accessed January 11, 2021. https://www.gilderlehrman.org/history-resources/teaching-resource/historical-context-facts-about-slave-trade-and-slavery

14. Higginbotham Jr., A. Leon. "Virginia Led the Way in Legal Oppression." *Washington Post.* May 21, 1978. https://www.washingtonpost.com/archive/opinions/1978/05/21/virginia-led-the-way-in-legal-oppression/664bcdf4-8aaf-475f-8ea7-eb597aee7ecd/

15. "Slave Law in Colonial Virginia: A Timeline." Sam Houston State University. Accessed January 11, 2021. https://www.shsu.edu/~jll004/vabeach course_spring09/bacons_rebellion/slavelawincolonialvirginiatimeline.pdf

16. Hutton, Clinton. "The Creative Ethos of the African Diaspora: Performance Aesthetics and the Fight for Freedom and Identity." *Caribbean Quarterly* 53, no. 1/2 (2007): 127-49. Accessed January 11, 2021. http://www.jstor.org/stable/40654979.

17. "United States Slavery Laws and Restrictions." Pure History. Accessed January 11, 2021. http://purehistory.org/united-states-slavery-laws-and-restrictions/

18. "Slave Law in Colonial Virginia: A Timeline." Sam Houston State University. Accessed January 11, 2021. https://www.shsu.edu/~jll004/vabeach course_spring09/bacons_rebellion/slavelawincolonialvirginiatimeline.pdf

19. Ruane, Michael E. "Freedom and Slavery, the Central Paradox of American History." *Washington Post.* April 30, 2019. https://www.washingtonpost.com/local/freedom-and-slavery-the-central-paradox-of-american-history/2019/04/30/16063754-2e3a-11e9-813a-0ab2f17e305b_story.html

20. Campell, Randolph B. "Slavery." Texas State Historical Association: Handbook of Texas. Accessed January 20, 2021. https://www.tshaonline.org/handbook/entries/slavery

21. Perea, Juan. "The Proslavery Constitution." American Constitution Society Expert Forum Law and Policy Analysis. February 1, 2016. https://www.acslaw.org/expertforum/the-proslavery-constitution/

22. Campell, Randolph B. "Slavery." Texas State Historical Association: Handbook of Texas. Accessed January 20, 2021. https://www.tshaonline.org/handbook/entries/slavery

23. "Interview with Felicia Furman." Reparations 4 Slavery. Accessed January 20, 2021. https://reparations4slavery.com/interview-with-felicia-furman/

24. Furman, Felicia. *Shared History.* Itvs.org. February 1, 2006. https://itvs.org/films/shared-history

25. Jones, John W. "Confederate Currency: The Color of Money Depictions of Slavery in Confederate and Southern States Currency." Accessed January 20, 2021. http://colorsofmoney.com/

26. Jones, Kimberly L. "Kimberly Latrice Jones BLM Video Speech Transcript." Rev.com. June 8, 2020. https://www.rev.com/blog/transcripts/kimberly-latrice-jones-blm-video-speech-transcript

27. "Shocking List of 10 Companies that Profited from the Slave Trade." Racism. Org. Accessed January 20, 2021. https://www.racism.org/index.php/articles/law-and-justice/citizenship-rights/117-slavery-to-reparations/reparations/1697-reparations1001

28. Thomas, Zoe. "The Hidden Links Between Slavery and Wall Street." BBC News. August 28, 2019. https://www.bbc.com/news/business-49476247

29. "Watch Night." Britannica. Accessed January 20, 2021. https://www.britannica.com/topic/Watch-Night

30. Davis, Michael. "National Archives Safeguards Original Juneteenth General Order." Archives.gov. Accessed January 20, 2021. https://www.archives.gov/news/articles/juneteenth-original-document#:~:text=Gordon%20Granger%20issued%20General%20Order,in%20Galveston%20the%20previous%20day.&text=This%20day%20has%20come%20to,combination%20of%20June%20and%20nineteenth

31. Nittle, Nadra K. "The Black Codes and Why They Still Matter Today." ThoughtCo. December 21, 2020. https://www.thoughtco.com/the-black-codes-4125744

32. "The Southern Black Codes of 1865-66." Constitutional Rights Foundation. Accessed January 20, 2021. https://www.crf-usa.org/brown-v-board-50th-anniversary/southern-black-codes.html

33. "Mississippi Black Codes (1865)." Facing History and Ourselves. Accessed January 20, 2021. https://www.facinghistory.org/reconstruction-era/mississippi-black-codes-1865

34. Ibid.

35. "Difference Between Black Codes and Jim Crow Laws." Difference.guru. February 2, 2018. https://difference.guru/difference-between-black-codes-and-jim-crow-laws/

36. "Mississippi Black Codes (1865)." Facing History and Ourselves. Accessed January 20, 2021. https://www.facinghistory.org/reconstruction-era/mississippi-black-codes-1865

37. "The Southern Black Codes of 1865-66." Constitutional Rights Foundation. Accessed January 20, 2021. https://www.crf-usa.org/brown-v-board-50th-anniversary/southern-black-codes.html

38. Tarter, Brent. "Vagrancy Act of 1866." Encyclopedia Virginia. Accessed February 4, 2021. https://www.encyclopediavirginia.org/Vagrancy_Act_of_1866#:~:text=The%20Vagrancy%20Act%20of%201866,to%20be%20unemployed%20or%20homeless.&text=It%20is%20unknown%20to%20what,law%20in%20Virginia%20until%201904

39. Schultz, Marisa. "Robert Johnson's Big Idea: $14 Trillion in Slavery Reparations to African-Americans." Fox. June 26, 2020. https://www.foxnews.com/politics/robert-johnsons-big-idea-14-trillion-slavery-reparations-payments-to-african-americans

40. Seitles, Marc. "The Perpetuation of Residential Racial Segregation in America: Historical Discrimination, Modern Forms of Exclusion, and Inclusionary

Remedies." *Florida State University Journal of Land Use and Environmental Law* 14, no. 1 (2018): 3.https://ir.law.fsu.edu/cgi/viewcontent.cgi?article=1191& context=jluel

41. Peters, Chloe. "Looking Back to Move Forward." *Monitor.* December 9, 2020. https://www.monitorsaintpaul.com/stories/looking-back-to-move-forward,1842

42. "Racial Restrictive Covenants." Seattle Civil Rights & Labor History Project, University of Washington. Accessed January 24, 2020. https://depts .washington.edu/civilr/covenants.htm

43. "Mapping Prejudice." University of Minnesota Data & Maps. Accessed January 24, 2021. https://mappingprejudice.umn.edu/data-and-map-launch-page/ index.html

44. Faber, Jacob W. "We Built This: Consequences of New Deal Era Intervention in America's Racial Geography." *American Sociological Review* 85, no. 5 (2020): 739-775. https://journals.sagepub.com/doi/full/10.1177/0003122420948464

45. Mitchell, Bruce, and Juan Franco. "HOLC 'Redlining' Maps: The Persistent Structure of Segregation and Economic Inequality." National Community Reinvestment Coalition. March 20, 2018. https://ncrc.org/holc/

46. Gopal, Keerti. "Generations of Pain: The Road to Reparations in Evanston." *Daily Northwestern.* May 29, 2020. https://dailynorthwestern.com/2020/05/29/ city/generations-of-pain-the-road-to-reparations-in-evanston/

47. Breen, Deborah. "Mapping Inequality: Redlining in New Deal America; Renewing Inequality: Family Displacements through Urban Renewal." (2019): 548-550. https://dsl.richmond.edu/panorama/redlining/#loc=5/39.1/-94.58

48. Moore, Natalie. "The Enduring Message on Home Ownership of 'It's a Wonderful Life.'" *Chicago Sun Times.* December 17, 2020. https://chicago .suntimes.com/columnists/2020/12/17/22180289/its-a-wonderful-life-frank- capra-christmas-home-ownership-working-class-natalie-moore

49. Mock, Brentin. "White Americans' Hold on Wealth Is Old, Deep, and Nearly Unshakeable." Bloomberg. September 3, 2019. https://www.bloom berg.com/news/articles/2019-09-03/the-amazing-resiliency-of-white-wealth

50. Osterland, Andrew. "What the Coming $68 Trillion Great Wealth Transfer Means for Financial Advisors." CNBC. October 21, 2019. https://www .cnbc.com/2019/10/21/what-the-68-trillion-great-wealth-transfer-means- for-advisors.html#:~:text=Cerulli%20Associates%20estimates%20that%20 as,after%20inheriting%20their%20parents'%20wealth.

51. Sullivan, Paul. "The Estate Tax May Change Under Biden, Affecting Far More People." *New York Times.* January 15, 2021. https://www.nytimes .com/2021/01/15/your-money/estate-tax-biden.html

52. Harris, Adam. "White College Graduates Are Doing Great with Their Parents' Money." *Atlantic*. July 20, 2018. https://www.theatlantic.com/education/archive/2018/07/black-white-wealth-gap-inheritance/565640/

53. Winslow, Olivia. "Long Island: Divided." Projects.anmy.com. November 17, 2019. https://projects.amny.com/long-island/segregation-real-estate-history/

54. Blakemore, Erin. "How the GI Bill's Promise Was Denied to a Million Black WWII Veterans." History News Network. June 24, 2019. https://historynewsnetwork.org/article/172344

55. Shiedower, Noah. "The Controversial History of Levittown, America's First Suburb." Untapped New York, July 31, 2020. https://untappedcities.com/2020/07/31/the-controversial-history-of-levittown-americas-first-suburb/

56. Sheyner, Gennady. "Housing's troubled history of discrimination." *Palo Alto Weekly*. March 29, 2019. https://www.paloaltoonline.com/news/2019/03/29/housings-troubled-history-of-discrimination

57. Shapiro, Ari. "'The Color of Law' Details How U.S. Housing Policies Created Segregation." NPR. May 17, 2017. https://www.npr.org/2017/05/17/528822128/the-color-of-law-details-how-u-s-housing-policies-created-segregation

58. Mista, Tanvi. "It Could Take 2 Centuries for Racial Wealth Disparities to Dissipate." Bloomberg. August 9, 2016. https://www.bloomberg.com/news/articles/2016-08-09/new-study-finds-wealth-disparities-between-races-widening-in-u-s

CHAPTER THREE

Donate to HBCUs

I am asking you to help close the Black-White wealth gap by donating at least 8.46% of your annual philanthropic giving to one or more HBCUs for the next five years.

"GET YOUR EDUCATION. It's the only thing they can't take away from you." These were the words of Zach Hubert Sr., a former slave, speaking to his 12 children.

In 2020, I visited 10 of the 101 HBCUs located in 19 states across the country, as seen in Figure 3.1. (The original schedule was to visit 12, but 2 were cancelled due to COVID-19.) I taught a workshop entitled "Entrepreneurial Finance for Black Entrepreneurs." It was one of the greatest, most enjoyable experiences of my teaching career. I got the opportunity to teach almost 700 Black students about brilliant Black entrepreneurs who were enormously successful as businessmen and -women, as

SUMMARY - HBCU TOUR

1. HOWARD UNIVERSITY...WASHINGTON, DC
   ◦ Enrollment: 6,200*
2. MORGAN STATE UNIVERSITY..................................BALTIMORE, MD
   ◦ Enrollment: 6,400
3. SPELMAN COLLEGE..ATLANTA, GA
   ◦ Enrollment: 2,100
4. BETHUNE-COOKMAN UNIVERSITY...............DAYTONA BEACH, FL
   ◦ Enrollment: 3,600
5. STILLMAN COLLEGE...TUSCALOOSA, AL
   ◦ Enrollment: 800
6. LINCOLN UNIVERSITY MISSOURI...................JEFFERSON CITY, MO
   ◦ Enrollment: 2,300
7. LINCOLN UNIVERSITY..............................LINCOLN UNIVERSITY, PA
   ◦ Enrollment: 2,400
8. BENNETT COLLEGE...GREENSBORO, NC
   ◦ Enrollment: 465
9. NORTH CAROLINA CENTRAL UNIVERSITY.................DURHAM, NC
   ◦ Enrollment: 6,400
10. CHICAGO STATE UNIVERSITY..............................CHICAGO, IL
    ◦ Enrollment: 2,000
11. DILLARD UNIVERSITY**..NEW ORLEANS, LA
    ◦ Enrollment: 1,300
12. HAMPTON UNIVERSITY**.......................................HAMPTON, VA
    ◦ Enrollment: 3,700

*Enrollment numbers are full-time, undergraduate students
**Cancelled due to COVID-19

Figure 3.1   Summary, HBCU Tour.

well as hugely successful at giving back, philanthropically, to the Black community. I use the colleges I visited as a subset of the broader discussion of the current state of HBCUs. (When one of my friends saw the map, he said it looked like a map of stops along the Underground Railroad, a consequence of the fact that I had visited several HBCUs in the deep South, as well as the northern part of the country.)

One of my major takeaways from this tour was that the HBCU coalition should be given a special award similar to the MacArthur "genius grant" for the exemplary and phenomenal work that they have done for this country and for the Black community. These colleges and universities, which were founded as early as the 1830s, were created to serve Black students when White colleges and universities denied admission to Blacks based solely on their race. Many of these schools were founded by and/or named after White religious leaders, military leaders, politicians, or philanthropists. For example, Spelman is the middle name of philanthropist Laura Rockefeller; Morehouse was renamed after Henry Morehouse, the White secretary of the National Baptist Home Missionary Society; and Stillman College, founded nearly a century and a half ago, in Tuscaloosa, Alabama, was named after a White reverend, Charles Stillman, the former pastor of the first Presbyterian Church of Tuscaloosa.

In Stillman College's more recent history, Vivian Malone, the first Black woman to enroll at the University of Alabama (UA), lived there. Although a full-time student at the University of Alabama, for her own safety she did not live on campus. She lived at Stillman instead and was escorted to classes at UA by federal troops.[1] This followed the resistance of Alabama Governor George Wallace, who defended segregation by standing in the doorway of the enrollment office to block her from entering the building. President Kennedy ordered National Guard troops to escort Malone into the building. There were regular death and bomb threats made in protest of her integrating the school. Every day, a student driver, Mack Jones, drove her to the University of Alabama. After becoming the first Black student to graduate from the University, she and Mack Jones married. Governor Wallace apologized to Malone thirty years later, in 1996, when he presented her with the Lurleen B. Wallace Award for Courage, named after his deceased wife. Stillman College's other claim to fame is that former Secretary of State Condoleezza Rice lived there as a child. Her father, John Rice, was the Dean of Students.

Another university with the name of a famous politician is Lincoln University in Missouri. (It shares the name with another HBCU in Pennsylvania whose student body today is majority White.) Ann Walton Kroenke is an alum. She is from the Walmart family and is America's wealthiest HBCU alumna.

HBCUs Financial Need

While inclusion of Black students at Predominately White Institutions (PWI) is common today, accounting for over 90% of all Black college students, HBCUs remain as important today as they were over 150 years ago, when they primarily served former enslaved men and women.

However, the average endowment of HBCUs is a mere $12 million.[2] They desperately need your contributions. These schools have always been burdened with financial challenges primarily due to the financial circumstances of the students they serve. Over 70% of HBCU students receive Pell Grants from the federal government. For example, Shaw University in North Carolina is "lovingly known as the mother of the other HBCUs" as the first HBCU (1865) in the Southern states. About 80% of students at Shaw University are eligible to receive federal Pell-Grants.[3] Families with annual household income of $30,000 are eligible for the grant. This compares to 39% for all undergraduate students nationally. Compounding these facts, over 60% of HBCU students are first-generation college students (with neither parent possessing a college degree), compared to 33% of students nationally and 15% of students at Ivy League schools.[4]

As observed by economist William Spriggs, "zero dollars is the maximum amount that over 60% of families of HBCU students can contribute to their child's education."[5] As I stated in Chapter 1, my family fell into that category. Thus, if HBCUs did not exist, most of their 300,000 students would likely not attend college. PWIs do not want an abundance of first-generation students from low-income families because they would require more financial assistance.

As Figure 3.2 shows, Black students have a greater reliance on loans than White students do.[6] Figure 3.3 illustrates that HBCU students use federal loans to borrow two times that

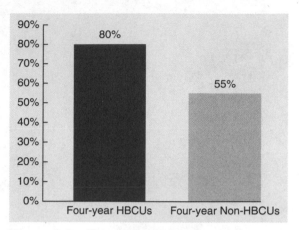

Figure 3.2   Percentage of undergraduates receiving a federal loan.

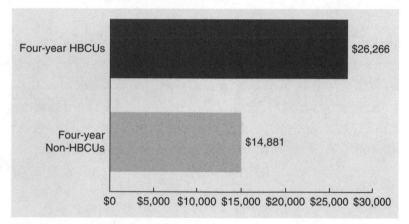

Figure 3.3   Median cumulative amount of federal loans borrowed by bachelor's degree recipients.

borrowed by non-HBCU students.[7] Figure 3.4 illustrates that the number of large-dollar borrowers ($40,000 or more) was four times higher for HBCU students than for non-HBCU students, and finally, the chart also shows that HBCU students were less likely to borrow zero dollars (i.e., no federal loans) than were non-HBCU students.

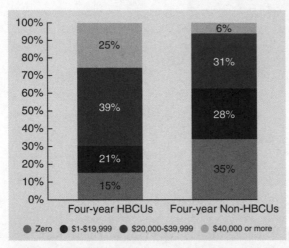

Figure 3.4   Distribution of cumulative federal loan debt for bachelor's degree recipients.

Despite the daunting financial picture of a student body short on economic resources or academic legacy, through dogged determination HBCUs have survived and strived to provide outstanding education to some of America's greatest leaders, including Dr. Martin Luther King Jr. and Supreme Court Justice Thurgood Marshall. Table 3.1 lists other celebrated HBCU alums.[8]

Endowments

One of the most important financial health metrics for a college or university is the size of its endowment. Endowments are charitable donations of money or other financial assets (e.g., stock, real estate, works of art). Typically, endowment funds have strict investment and disbursement criteria imposed by the donors. The intent of endowments is to act as "rainy day funds," but also to fund specific initiatives such as fellowships, professorships, scholarships, and student financial aid. Investment guidelines on how investment income can be spent usually identify 5% of the

Table 3.1   Prominent HBCU alumni

	Name	HBCU	Comments
1	Yolanda Adams	Texas Southern University	• Grammy Award–winning gospel singer
2	Anthony Anderson	Howard University	• Actor, comedian, writer; star of the show *Blackish*
3	Namadi Azikwe	Lincoln University of Pennsylvania	• Politician; first president of Nigeria
4	Erykah Badu	Grambling State University	• Named the First Lady of Neo-Soul
5	Chadwick Boseman	Howard University	• Actor; especially known for the movie *Black Panther*
6	Toni Braxton	Bowie State University	• Singer, songwriter, actress, TV personality
7	Rosalind Brewer	Spelman College	• COO, Starbucks • Former president and CEO, Sam's Club
8	Common	Florida A&M University	• Grammy Award–winning artist
9	Marian Wright Edelman	Spelman College	• Founder and president of Children's Defense Fund
10	Roberta Flack	Howard University	• R&B singer
11	Earl Graves	Morgan State University	• Publisher and founder, *Black Enterprise* magazine

(Continued)

Table 3.1 (Continued)

	Name	HBCU	Comments
12	Alex Haley	Alcorn State University	• Writer, author of *The Autobiography of Malcolm X* and 1977 Pulitzer Prize winner for *Roots*
13	Taraji P. Henson	Howard University	• Actress
14	Rev. Jesse Jackson	North Carolina A&T State University	• Civil Rights activist
15	Randy Jackson	Southern University of Baton Rouge	• Singer, record producer, TV personality
16	Samuel L. Jackson	Morehouse College	• Actor and producer
17	Spike Lee	Morehouse College	• Film director, producer, screenwriter
18	Reginald Lewis	Virginia State University	• First African American to build a billion-dollar company
19	Eva Marcille	Clark Atlanta University	• Fashion model, winner of *America's Next Top Model*, Season 3
20	Toni Morrison	Howard University	• Author; 1987 Pulitzer Prize winner for *Beloved* • First Black woman awarded the Nobel Prize in Literature, in 1993

Table 3.1 (Continued)

	Name	HBCU	Comments
21	Marilyn Mosby	Tuskegee University	• State attorney for Baltimore
22	Kweisi Mfume	Morgan State University	• U.S. Representative for Maryland's 7th Congressional District • Former president and CEO, NAACP
23	Kwame Nkrumah	Lincoln University of Pennsylvania	• First prime minister and president of Ghana
24	Pam Oliver	Florida A&M University	• Sportscaster for NBA and NFL
25	Phylicia Rashad	Howard University	• Actress; known for *The Cosby Show*
26	Kasim Reed	Howard University	• Former mayor of Atlanta
27	Jerry Rice	Mississippi Valley State University	• Former wide receiver, San Francisco 49ers
28	Lionel Richie	Tuskegee University	• Singer, songwriter, producer
29	Anika Noni Rose	Florida A&M University	• Actress; voiced Tiana in *The Princess and the Frog,* Disney's first African American princess
30	Stephen Smith	Winston-Salem State University	• Sports journalist, NBA analyst on SportsCenter

(Continued)

Table 3.1   (Continued)

	Name	HBCU	Comments
31	Michael Strahan	Texas Southern University	• TV host, journalist • Former New York Giants defensive
32	Wanda Sykes	Hampton University	• Actress and comedian
33	John Thompson	Florida A&M University	• Independent chairman of Microsoft Corp.
34	Alice Walker	Spelman College	• Author; 1983 Pulitzer Prize winner for novel *The Color Purple*
35	Oprah Winfrey	Tennessee State University	• Talk show host, television producer, philanthropist

endowment's total asset value. The larger the endowment's asset value, the greater the amount of funds available.

HBCU endowment funding has historically lagged the funding of PWIs. As stated in a 2017 Bloomberg article, of the 90 schools with billion-dollar endowments not one is an HBCU.[9] As of 2019, Howard University in Washington, D.C., had the largest HBCU endowment at approximately $693 million. Howard is ranked 160th on Bloomberg's list, while Harvard is number one at roughly $40 billion. The total endowment of all HBCUs as of 2019 was $2.1 billion, or approximately 5% of Harvard alone. And 54 PWIs have endowments of at least $2 billion. Even in the "business" of education, the wealth gap rears its menacing head.

The average HBCU alumni giving is about 11.2%. There are four HBCUs where alumni giving exceeded 30%: Claflin

University, Spelman College, Bennett College, and Lane College.[10] The average alumni giving rate for all colleges is about 11.6%,[11] but in the top tier the alumni donations range from 22% to 48%.[12] With less generational wealth, alumni of HBCUs do not have the same level of discretionary income to donate as alums of PWIs. For example, as of 2018, Harvard had 188 alumni who were billionaires.[13] In contrast, within the HBCU coalition, there are only two billionaires, Oprah Winfrey and Ann Walton Kroenke (yes, a Walton from Walmart, and, yes, she is White).[14]

The financial challenges of HBCUs are not limited to endowments. For example, in a 2018 study by the *Journal of Financial Economics*, it was determined that HBCUs pay higher underwriting fees to issue tax-exempt bonds compared to non-HBCUs. According to researchers, "This appears to reflect higher costs of finding willing buyers: the effect is three times larger in the far Deep South, where racial animus remains the most severe. Credit quality plays little role. For example, identical differences are observed between HBCU and non HBCUs: 1) with AAA ratings, and/or 2) insured by the same company, even before the 2008 Financial Crisis. HBCU-issued bonds are also more expensive to trade in secondary markets, and when they do, sit in dealer inventory longer."[15]

These types of anti-Black practices must be stopped. One idea is for the government to use the "carrot, not the stick" model of positive incentives. If that does not work, the strategy is to make it expensive to practice anti-Black discrimination. For example, in March 2020, the State of Maryland settled with Maryland HBCUs for $577 million in racial discrimination compensation.[16] It must be noted that the four universities (Bowie State, Coppin State, Morgan State, and Maryland Eastern Shore) were in litigation for more than a decade.

Speaking of a winning strategy, let's return to the Hubert Family. Zach Hubert Sr. was taught to read by the plantation owner's son. This was in violation of laws forbidding teaching enslaved Black people how to read. After gaining their freedom, Mr. Hubert Sr. and his wife saved enough money to buy some land, where they earned a living as farmers. They built a school and hired a teacher to instruct their 12 children, all of whom attended college. Two attended Massachusetts Agricultural College, which is now the University of Massachusetts Amherst. Ten graduated from Morehouse or Spelman College, and Zach Hubert Jr. would go on to be president of Jackson College in Jackson, Mississippi. Now that is Black excellence!

HBCU History

Originally, the primary mission of HBCUs was to teach and prepare formerly enslaved and free Black people the skills for gainful employment. The oldest HBCU, originally named the African Institute and now known as Cheyney University, was founded by Richard Humphreys in 1837 in Pennsylvania. Humphreys, a White Quaker philanthropist, bequeathed $10,000, one-tenth of his estate, to design and establish a school for people of African descent. During the 1850s, three more HBCUs were founded: Miner Normal School (1851) in Washington, D.C., Lincoln University (1854) in Pennsylvania, and Wilberforce (1856) in Ohio. The African Methodist Episcopal Church established Wilberforce University, the first HBCU operated by Blacks.

The majority of HBCUs originated between 1865 and 1900, with the greatest number founded in 1867, two years after the Emancipation Proclamation. Those schools were Alabama State University, Barber-Scotia College, Fayetteville State University, Howard University, Johnson C. Smith University, Morehouse

College, Morgan State University, Saint Augustine's University, and Talladega College.

The federal government, via the Freedman's Bureau, played a critical role in the rapid expansion of HBCUs. The impact of the Freedman's Bureau is a clear example of government policies that worked for its targeted audience. The Freedmen's Bureau, formally known as the Bureau of Refugees, Freedmen and Abandoned Lands, was established in 1865 by Congress and President Abraham Lincoln to help millions of former Black enslaved people and poor Whites in the South in the aftermath of the Civil War. This government agency provided food, housing, medical aid, and legal assistance to newly freed Black citizens. It also created schools. The first commissioner of the Freedman's Bureau was General Otis Howard, an officer of the Union Army. He also founded Howard University with funding from the Freedman's Bureau.

During its years of operation from 1865 until 1872, the bureau was instrumental in building 3,000 free schools, and helped found HBCUs, such as Fisk University in Nashville, Tennessee, and Hampton University in Hampton, Virginia. Like Howard University, these schools also had a close relationship with the Union military. Fisk is named after General Clinton Fisk, and General Samuel Armstrong was the first president of Hampton.

In the summer of 1872, Congress dismantled the Freedman's Bureau due to pressure from White southerners.[17] Despite the termination of this government agency that supported education for Black Americans, the number of HBCUs continued to grow in number and importance. For example, after the country's victory in WWII, many veterans used the G.I. Bill benefits to pay for their college tuition and living expenses. This pursuit of higher education was instrumental in developing America's new middle class. Altogether, 7.8 million servicemen and servicewomen were educated under the G.I. Bill, but one must remember that the one million Black veterans of the war could not attend PWIs despite honorably serving their country.[18] Shockingly, former enemy German soldiers could come to America and attend PWIs because they were White. Conversely, Black military veterans could only matriculate at HBCUs. The number of Black veterans attending HBCUs increased from 1.08% of total U.S. college enrollment in 1940 to 3.6% in 1950.[19] But those schools were so small and over-crowded that they could not accommodate the entire estimated 100,000 Black veterans who had applied to college through the G.I. Bill. By 1946, only 20,000 of those applicants had regis-tered at HBCUs.[20]

Despite being only 3% of the colleges or universities in the United States, the 101 schools that are classified as HBCUs have produced one U.S. vice president, 80% of Black judges, 50% of Black lawyers, 50% of Black doctors, 40% of Black engineers, 40% of the Black members of Congress, and 13% of the Black CEOs in America today.[21] This is further evidence of the impor-tance of HBCUs to America.

Science has historically been a pillar of the HBCU cur-riculum. The successful integration of this academic focus at HBCUs can best be highlighted by looking at Black undergradu-ates from 2002 to 2011 who continued to get PhDs in STEM subject areas. Howard University produced 220 STEM doctor-ates, while Stanford, Harvard, MIT, and Yale combined to pro-duce 221 such Black PhDs.[22] Two HBCU alums with STEM degrees are Lonnie Johnson and Katherine Johnson (not related). Katherine Johnson majored in mathematics at West Virginia State University. Her brilliance as a mathematician was highlighted in the film *Hidden Figures*. As a NASA employee, she successfully calculated the orbital mechanics that resulted in the safe return of the country's first spaceship occupied by an astronaut. Like Katherine Johnson, Lonnie Johnson worked for NASA, where he was an engineer after receiving his master's degree in nuclear engineering from Tuskegee University. He has over 100 patents and is most famous for inventing the Super Soaker water gun.

Two Lincoln Universities

I always knew that there was an HBCU named after President Abraham Lincoln, but until I began planning my tour of HCBUs I was oblivious to the fact that there are two separate schools with the same name. The name Lincoln was selected in the 1860s as an homage to the president who signed the Emancipation Proclamation. In addition to a shared name, there are other similarities between these schools. Both have small enrollments of fewer than 5,000 students and are located in rural communities, with beautiful campuses. However, there are striking differences between the two schools.

One university was founded north of the Mason-Dixon line (Pennsylvania), the other was founded south of the Mason-Dixon line (Missouri). One was "public and state-related" (Pennsylvania) and the other was established with financial donations from members of two Colored Infantry units of the Union Army (Missouri). One is historically and predominately Black (Pennsylvania) the other is historically Black and currently predominately non-Black (Missouri). The 2019 fall enrollment of this university is 57% non-Black and 43% Black. In looking at the data since 1995, non-Black enrollment has been as high as 75%. I became aware of this development after I scheduled my visit to the school. I received a call from one of the deans who told me how elated he was that I had included Lincoln University on my list and that the students were looking forward to my visit. He then continued to tell me that the school might look a little different from the other HBCUs on my tour. Specifically, aside from the beautiful bronze statue at the center of campus depicting the Black soldiers from the Civil War who founded the school in 1866, the school's faculty, students, and surrounding community might give one the impression that it is a PWI. He wanted to ensure me that it was indeed an HBCU.

So how could a college that was founded by Black veterans of the American Civil war come to have a majority White student body? Well, HBCUs have always welcomed students of all races. Dr. King stated it best in 1957 when he said, "Although Negro colleges are by and large segregated institutions, they are not segregating institutions."[23]

The other Lincoln University, situated outside of Philadelphia, was founded by Quakers in 1854 and was the first HBCU to award a college degree. It too has a fascinating history. During its early years, Lincoln was known colloquially as the "Black Princeton" due to its Princeton University–educated founder and early faculty, rigorous classical curriculum ties to the Presbyterian Church, and its similarities in school colors (orange and black for Princeton; orange and blue for Lincoln) and mascots (tiger for Princeton; lion for Lincoln). While Lincoln does not have Princeton's multi-billion-dollar endowment, Lincoln's $42 million endowment as of June 30, 2018, is over 200% greater than the average for HBCUs. But the school still requires financial assistance. An endowment of this size only produces $2 million annually for spending if we apply the 5% rule for endowment spending.

Two of Lincoln University's most famous alums are the great poet Langston Hughes and Thurgood Marshall, the first Black person to serve on the Supreme Court of the United States. Another important alum was Dr. Horace Mann Bond, the school's first Black president. He was also the father of the great Civil Rights leader Julian Bond. Dr. Bond befriended Dr. Albert Barnes, a White businessman, who helped Lincoln University build the beautiful campus that I saw during my visit.

Barnes was a generous man with a keen intellect and a sharp business sense, who also believed in equal rights and opportunities for Black people. He grew up in a blue-collar family, in a poverty-stricken area of Philadelphia. In his youth his mother, a devout Methodist, took him to church camps and revivals that included Black people. These early experiences set the stage for his progressive worldview and allowed him to empathize and identify with the struggle of Black people in America. At 17, he graduated from high school and went on to medical school at the University of Pennsylvania. He supported himself during this period by tutoring, boxing, and playing semiprofessional baseball. He continued his education with postgraduate training in pharmacology and chemistry in Germany. Upon his return to the States, in 1899, he formed a partnership with another chemist, Herman Hille. Their partnership created Argyrol, a silver nitrate antiseptic used to prevent newborn infant blindness. In 1908, their company dissolved, and Barnes formed his own company, A.C. Barnes Company, which he sold just before the stock market crash of 1929. This move allowed him to retain his fortune. As an entrepreneur, he had a company with employees of different races. This made him different, and he loved being different. Barnes created a six-hour workday for his employees, with two additional voluntary hours for educational classes. He brought in educators and lecturers to teach a wide range of topics on race, injustice, and psychology. Barnes provided pensions for his employees and their widows. His "wokeness" was evident in the treatment of his Black employees, through his hiring, and assisting them to purchase homes, skirting discriminatory housing practices. His feelings about anti-Black discrimination were clearly expressed in 1925, in his essay entitled "Negro Art in America," which stated:

> The emancipation of the Negro slave in America gave him only a nominal freedom. Like all other human beings, he is a creature of habits which tie him to his past; equally set are his white brothers' habits toward him. The relationship of master and slave has changed but little in the sixty years of freedom. He is still a slave to the ignorance, the prejudice, the cruelty which were the fate of his forefathers. To-day he has not yet found a place of equality in the social, educational or industrial world of the white man.[24]

Barnes began collecting art in 1911, which became a full-time passion after he sold his company. Through the help of one of his high school friends, William Glackens, a prominent artist, he became aware of an emerging trend in art from Europe called Post-Impressionism. Barnes became enthralled by the works of Pablo Picasso, Pierre-Auguste Renoir, Paul Cézanne, and Henri Matisse, so much so that he amassed the largest collection of Post-Impressionist art in the world. He wanted to share his artwork with people from all walks of life, and in 1922, he formed an educational foundation, the Barnes Foundation. As the foundation grew, so did the types of art he acquired and presented. Barnes was one of the first people in the art world to procure African Art and support Black artists such as Horace Pippen. As the mainstream art world caught up with his tastes, he became more guarded and focused on his mission to educate the world via art, contesting its commercialization. He also detested the White elite art critics in Philadelphia. At one time, they criticized his collection and the way that it was displayed.

As the Barnes Foundation continued to grow during the 1930s and '40s, so did the value of the foundation's collection. In his will, Barnes assigned Lincoln University the right to nominate four of the foundation's five directors, effectively giving Lincoln University control of the foundation.[25] Tragically, he died in a car accident in 1951. Upon his death, his wife controlled the Barnes Foundation. They had no children, and when his wife died, the control of the Barnes art collection was in the hands of Lincoln University. When this fact was publicized, it shocked the arts world. The collection had over 4,000 pieces of art, including 181 works by Pierre-Auguste Renoir, 69 works by Paul Cézanne, 59 works by Henri Matisse, and 46 works by Pablo Picasso.[26]

The estimated value of the collection was $25 billion and an HBCU with just 1,300 students controlled it! On October 19, 1989, a *New York Times* headline read, "Small University Gains Control of the Barnes Foundation."[27] A year earlier, on September 27, 1988, a *Philadelphia Inquirer* headline had read, "Lincoln U to Control $1 billion art collection."[28] The article stated, "Months before his death in 1951, Dr. Albert C. Barnes removed the Pennsylvania Academy of Fine Arts and the University of Pennsylvania, and instead designated Lincoln University, a small, obscure, historically Black college to appoint trustees to the foundation."

Barnes had some very specific language in his trust that greatly influenced what Lincoln University could and could not do with the artwork after he passed away. He had specific provisions around how the art was to be displayed, that it was not to be sold, lent, or have anything added to it. He also specified that no "functions" outside of classes (i.e., society events, museum-type exhibitions, etc.) would be allowed at the foundation. He also said that no color reproductions of the paintings would be allowed. A $10 million endowment was left to manage the operations of the foundation, which proved to be a woefully inadequate sum for Lincoln University to legally defend Barnes's will. Ultimately, the governor and the attorney general of Pennsylvania pressured Lincoln University to give up control of the Barnes Foundation. They wanted to display the art in downtown Philadelphia, and in essence, they found a way to break Barnes's will. Financially, Lincoln University had no recourse but to concede. Barnes left no money for them to fight lawsuits and, as stated in the movie *The Art of the Steal*, the aforementioned government officials were making threats to Lincoln University. Thus, Lincoln University agreed to a proposal that increased the number of seats on the board to 15 from the original 5. The result was that Lincoln held only 4 of the 15 board seats. The new members quickly voted to move the art collection from its suburban location to a new museum in downtown Philadelphia.

While Lincoln University lost the management of the Barnes Foundation (remember, they never owned the art collection), their agreement with the Commonwealth of Pennsylvania dramatically improved their campus, contributing to almost doubling their student enrollment. The Commonwealth invested over $125 million into Lincoln University via Capital Spending Bill H.B. 1634 for 2003–04.[29]

Recent Donations

In wake of the 2020 murders of Breonna Taylor, Ahmaud Arbery, and George Floyd, along with the subsequent social unrest, many White people decided to take action to be a part of the solution to the Black-White wealth gap problem in America. Such action seemed to be part of their answer to the question "How did we get into this mess?"

One response to "What can we do?" was the rise of a new generation of philanthropists who have made large donations to

HBCUs. Reed Hastings, CEO of Netflix, pledged $120 million to Spelman College, Morehouse College, and the United Negro College Fund. This gift is the largest-ever contribution from an individual in support of scholarships at an HBCU. An example of the impact is that at least 200 first-year students will be able to attend Morehouse and graduate debt free.

MacKenzie Scott (formerly Bezos) donated $150 million to Hampton University, Howard University, Morehouse College, Spelman College, Tuskegee University, and Xavier University. Scott has an estimated net worth around $60 billion and pledged to give most of her wealth away during her lifetime by focusing on nine areas of need, which include racial equality.[30]

Additional scholarship donations have been made by several other hedge fund and private equity investors. Seth Klarman, co-founder of the Baupost Group hedge fund, donated $10 million to Spelman to support student scholarships.[31] Frank Baker, a Black man who is the founder and managing partner of Siris private equity, donated $1 million toward the establishment of scholarships at Spelman.[32]

Michael Bloomberg, former mayor of New York, has pledged $100 million to four historically Black medical schools (Meharry Medical College, Howard University College of Medicine, Morehouse School of Medicine, and Charles R. Drew University of Medicine and Science) as part of his Greenwood Initiative.[33] Bloomberg named the initiative after the Greenwood community of Tulsa, Oklahoma, which was destroyed by White racists in the infamous "Black Wall Street Massacre" of 1921. The goal of the initiative is to reduce the debt burden of medical students at HBCUs. "By helping to train the next generation of Black doctors, this investment will save lives and begin to reduce the inequities in our health system that the current economic and public health crisis has underscored."

Oprah Winfrey has been a major contributor to HBCUs for the past few decades. She recently added $13 million to her Oprah Winfrey Scholars Program at Morehouse College, pushing her total investment to $25 million.[34] Altogether, she has donated almost $30 million to HBCUs. In 2020, she came to the aid of her alma mater, Tennessee State, and the surrounding community with a donation of $2 million to help offset the effects of COVID-19 on the university and the local business community.[35]

The Vista Equity CEO, Robert F. Smith, who is currently the richest Black man in America, proclaimed at the 2019 commencement of Morehouse College that the class of 2019 was "his," meaning that he was personally claiming the graduating seniors as his own and that he and his family would make a grant to eliminate their student loans.[36] On that day, 396 students heard that the burden on their ability to close the wealth gap shrank due to the benevolence of Robert Smith and his family.[37] Some of the Morehouse students interviewed after the announcement stated how fortunate they were to receive such a life-changing gift. One student said, "I could now apply to a wider range of medical schools because I have less school debt."

Corporations and organizations such as Dominion Energy and the Community Foundation of Greater Memphis have also made major donations to HBCUs. In July 2020, Dominion Energy, a public traded utility company based in Virginia, pledged $35 million to support HBCUs in the markets they serve: Virginia, Ohio, North Carolina, and South Carolina. Thomas F. Farrell, Dominion president and CEO, said at the time of the gift:

> We all know there are no actions or words that will immediately heal the hurt caused by four hundred years of institutional

racism. But since early June, we have seen signs of change and growth. Our country is moving forward. We are moving forward, too. This initiative is a recognition of the important role played by these institutions in African American advancement and the importance of education as an equalizer in society. These institutions have been foundational in the struggle to improve the lives of African Americans and in the fight for social justice. We are pleased and humbled to build on our company's nearly forty-year history of supporting historically black colleges and universities.[38]

That same month, LeMoyne-Owen College, in Memphis, Tennessee, was named the beneficiary of a $40 million endowment from the Community Foundation of Greater Memphis,[39] the largest endowment the school has ever received. The gift allows unrestricted use of the funds for the purposes determined by LeMoyne-Owen. Nearly 90% of its students qualify for financial aid or currently receive federal Pell Grants.

Even the Augusta National Golf Club, which hosts the prestigious Master's Tournament, stepped up with the funding of two scholarships at Paine College, called the Lee Elder scholarships. Almost a half century ago, Lee Elder was the first Black person to play in the Master's Tournament.[40]

The country club sport of golf and its participants made a "hole in one" when Master's winner and World Golf Hall of Famer Phil Mickelson donated $500,000 to Jackson State University in Mississippi,[41] ahead of a televised celebrity golf match with Stephen Curry of the NBA, Peyton Manning of the NFL, and Charles Barkley of the NBA that raised almost $4.4 million donated to 20 HBCUs.[42]

Charles Barkley has been a good friend to HBCUs, with $1 million each donated to Alabama A&M University, and Clark Atlanta University in 2016, $1 million to Morehouse College in 2017, and $1 million each to Miles College and Tuskegee University in 2020.[43]

How to Make Donations

Table 3.2 provides a list of HBCUs by state.[44] As you explore the different HBCU schools, consider their specialties and areas of strength and what a donation would mean in terms of the impact on the Black community. The president of Howard University, Dr. Wayne Fredrick, stated in an interview about this subject, "What's necessary is first to really find areas where we can have the biggest impact and make sure that we do that extremely well. That does require some focused funding in particular areas."[45] He went on to give an example about dentistry, noting that 40% of the Black dentists in this country are produced by two HBCU schools, Howard and Meharry Medical College. Funding programs that increase the quality of and access to programs like these could be exponentially beneficial. Find your school in the following ways:

- Research HBCU by state, academics, specialty, and focus areas.
- Find schools that align with your passions and interests.
- Contribute 8.46% of your philanthropic dollars to either the school's endowment or in support of specific programs.
- Design your contribution in a way that allows the HBCU to invest/disburse outside of industry norms (i.e., 5% of endowment used only for administrative purposes).

Table 3.2   HBCUs by state.

Alabama	Lawson State Community College	Philander Smith College	**Florida**	Fort Valley State University
Alabama A&M University	Miles College	Shorter College	Bethune-Cookman University	Interdenominational Theological Center
Alabama State University	Oakwood College	University of Arkansas at Pine Bluff	Edward Waters College	Morehouse College
Bishop State Community College	Selma University		Florida A&M University	Morehouse School of Medicine
C.A. Fredd Campus of Shelton State Community College	Stillman College	**Delaware**	Florida Memorial University	Morris Brown College
	Talladega College	Delaware State University		Paine College
Concordia College Selma	Trenholm State Technical College		**Georgia**	Savannah State University
Gadsden State Community College	Tuskegee University	**District of Columbia**	Albany State University	Spelman College
J. F. Drake Technical College	**Arkansas**	Howard University	Clark Atlanta University	**Kentucky**
	Arkansas Baptist College	University of the District of Columbia		Kentucky State University

(Continued)

Table 3.2 (Continued)

Louisiana	Morgan State University	Hinds Community College
Dillard University	University of Maryland, Eastern Shore	Jackson State University
Grambling State University	**Michigan**	Mississippi Valley State University
Southern University at New Orleans	Lewis College of Business	Rust College
Southern University at Shreveport	**Mississippi**	Tougaloo College
Xavier University of Louisiana	Alcorn State University	
Maryland	Coahoma Community College	**Missouri**
Bowie State University	Harris-Stowe State University	
Coppin State University	Lincoln University of Missouri	

North Carolina
Barber-Scotia College
Bennett College
Elizabeth City State University
Fayetteville State University
Johnson C. Smith University
Livingstone College
North Carolina A&T State University
North Carolina Central University
St. Augustine's College
Shaw University
Winston Salem State University
Ohio
Central State University
Wilberforce University
Oklahoma
Langston University

Table 3.2 (Continued)

Pennsylvania	Morris College	Tennessee State University	Southwestern Christian College	Virginia Union University
Cheyney University of Pennsylvania	Voorhees College	**Texas**	Texas College	Virginia University of Lynchburg
Lincoln University	**Tennessee**	Huston-Tillotson University	Texas Southern University	**West Virginia**
South Carolina	American Baptist College	Jarvis Christian College	Wiley College	Bluefield State College
Allen University	Fisk University	Paul Quinn College	**Virginia**	West Virginia State University
Benedict College	Knoxville College	Prairie View A&M University	Hampton University	**U.s. Virgin Islands**
Claflin University	Lane College	Saint Philip's College	Norfolk State University	University of the Virgin Islands
Clinton Junior College	LeMoyne-Owen College		Virginia State University	
Denmark Technical College	Meharry Medical College			

Schools That Are Not Colleges

While this chapter has been primarily devoted to HBCUs and college students, I believe it is important to ask for your financial support of any educational programs aimed at the Black community. One of the most significant primary and secondary programs was the Rosenwald School Project, which provided educational opportunities to poor Black students in the rural South.[46] The project was established in the early 20th century when there were not as many federally funded public schools for Black children. Two of the Rosenwald School's most famous alums are poet Maya Angelou and Congressman John Lewis.

The Rosenwald School Project was named after Julius Rosenwald, a Jewish-American clothier who was also a founder of Sears, Roebuck and Company. Rosenwald befriended Booker T. Washington, the founder of Tuskegee University, an HBCU. In 1912, Washington asked Rosenwald to join the board of Tuskegee, and through that relationship they started to build primary and secondary schools in rural Alabama. Subsequently, Rosenwald and his family established a charitable fund in 1917 that donated more than $70 million to public schools, colleges, universities, and Black institutions. The Rosenwald Fund, in collaboration with architects from Tuskegee Institute, then proceeded to build almost 5,000 schools in 15 Southern states.

By 1928, a third of the South's rural Black children and teachers were served by Rosenwald Schools. When *Brown v. Board of Education* became law and desegregation became a reality, the Rosenwald Schools became obsolete. In 2002, the National Trust, working with local officials and activists, placed the Rosenwald Schools on its list of the 11 Most Endangered Historic Places. A preservation project is still underway to ensure this monumental humanitarian effort is documented and preserved.

Notes

1. "Vivian Malone Jones." NAACP Legal Defense and Educational Fund, Inc. Accessed December 27, 2020. https://www.naacpldf.org/about-us/scholarship-recipients/vivian-malone-jones/#:~:text=Vivian%20Malone%20Jones%20became%20the,the%20National%20Honor%20Society%2C%20Ms

2. Smith, Kate. "Historically Black Colleges Try to Catch Up as Rich Schools Get Richer." *Bloomberg.* July 19, 2017. https://www.bloomberg.com/news/articles/2017-07-18/historically-black-colleges-try-to-catch-up-as-rich-schools-get-richer

3. St. Amour, Madeline. "HBCUs Grapple with Disparities." *Inside Higher Ed.* July 27, 2020. https://www.insidehighered.com/news/2020/07/27/financial-disparities-among-hbcus-and-between-sector-and-majority-white-institutions#:~:text=Dillard%20hopes%20Shaw's%20history%20as,other%20HBCUs%20in%20the%20South

4. "The HBCU Effect." United Negro College Fund. Accessed December 27, 2020. https://uncf.org/pages/the-hbcu-effect

5. Hall, Izzy. "Charitable Donations to HBCUs from Noted Philanthropists." Scholarships.com. August 6, 2020. https://www.scholarships.com/news/charitable-donations-to-HBCUs-from-noted-philanthropist

6. "Fewer Resources, More Debt: Loan Debt Burdens Students at Historically Black Colleges and Universities." United Negro College Fund. 2016. https://files.eric.ed.gov/fulltext/ED573646.pdf

7. "HBCU Students Are Burdened by Loan Debt; Policy Reforms Can Address Their Financial Challenges." United Negro College Fund. December 14, 2016. https://uncf.org/news/hbcu-students-are-burdened-by-loan-debt-policy-reforms-can-address-their-fi

8. HBCU alum list curated through Google search.

9. Smith, Kate. "Historically Black Colleges Try to Catch Up as Rich Schools Get Richer." *Bloomberg.* July 19, 2017. https://www.bloomberg.com/news/articles/2017-07-18/historically-black-colleges-try-to-catch-up-as-rich-schools-get-richer

10. "The Sorry State of Alumni Giving at Historically Black Colleges and Universities." *Journal of Blacks in Higher Education, U.S. News & World Report.* July 14, 2017. https://www.jbhe.com/2017/07/the-sorry-state-of-alumni-giving-at-historically-black-colleges-and-universities/

11. "10 Universities Where the Most Alumni Donate." *U.S. News & World Report.* June 18, 2018. https://wtop.com/news/2018/06/10-universities-where-the-most-alumni-donate-2/#:~:text=In%20that%20period%2C%20the%2010,roughly%2040%20percentage%20points%20lower

12. "Average Share of Alumni Who Donate to Their Alma Mater in the U.S. in 2019, by College." Statista. Accessed December 27, 2020. https://www.statista.com/statistics/1079276/average-share-alumni-donate-alma-mater-college-us/

13. https://www.cnbc.com/2018/05/18/the-universities-that-produce-the-most-billionaires.html#:~:text=Leading%20the%20way%20is%20Harvard,Stanford%2C%20MIT%20and%20Yale%20combined

14. "Who Is the Wealthiest HBCU Graduate? Hint: It Is Not Oprah Winfrey." HBCU Money. October 21, 2014. https://hbcumoney.com/2014/10/21/the-wealthiest-hbcu-graduate-hint-it-is-not-oprah-winfrey/

15. Dougal, Casey, Pengjie Gao, William J. Mayew, and Christopher A. Parsons. "What's in a (School) Name? Racial Discrimination in Higher Education Bond Markets." *Journal of Financial Economics* 134, no. 3 (2019): 570-590. https://www.sciencedirect.com/science/article/abs/pii/S0304405X19301242

16. "$577M Discrimination Settlement for Maryland HBCUs." USBE Online. March 28, 2020. https://www.blackengineer.com/article/577m-discrimination-settlement-for-maryland-hbcus/

17. "Freedman's Bureau." HISTORY.com. June 1, 2010, last modified October 3, 2018. https://www.history.com/topics/black-history/freedmens-bureau

18. Herbold, Hilary. "Never a Level Playing Field: Blacks and the GI Bill." *Journal of Blacks in Higher Education* 6 (1994): 104–108. https://www.jstor.org/stable/2962479?seq=1

19. "The First GI Bill and the Disparity for Black Veterans." Fight4Vets.com. Accessed December 27, 2020. https://fight4vets.com/the-first-gi-bill-and-the-disparity-for-black-veterans/

20. "The G.I. Bill of Rights." Lumen Learning. Accessed December 27, 2020. https://courses.lumenlearning.com/boundless-ushistory/chapter/culture-of-abundance/#:~:text=By%201946%2C%20only%20one%20fifth,away%20an%20estimated%2020%2C000%20veterans.

21. Hill, Jemele. "It's Time for Black Athletes to Leave White Colleges." *Atlantic*. October 2019. https://www.theatlantic.com/magazine/archive/2019/10/black-athletes-should-leave-White-colleges/596629/

22. Fiegener, Mark, and Steven Proudfoot. "Baccalaureate Origins of U.S.-trained S&E Doctorate Recipients." National Center for Science and Engineering Statistics. April 2013. https://www.nsf.gov/statistics/infbrief/nsf13323/nsf13323.pdf

23. Carswell. Shirley. "Five Myths About Historically Black Colleges and Universities." *Washington Post*. March 3, 2017. https://www.washingtonpost.com/opinions/five-myths-about-hbcus/2017/03/03/5adc236a-ff76-11e6-8f41-ea6ed597e4ca_story.html

24. Barnes, Albert C. "Negro Art and America." 1925. https://explorepahistory.com/odocument.php?docId=1-4-9C

25. "The Lincoln University-Barnes Foundation Relationship in Perspective: Lincoln University Acts to Protect Integrity of Responsibility for the Barnes Foundation." *Lincoln University Campus News*. January 19, 2002. https://www.lincoln.edu/new-and-events/news/lincoln-university-barnes-foundation-relationship-perspective-lincoln-university

26. "Lincoln University Unveils Historic Academic Partnership with the Barnes Foundation." *Lincoln University Campus News*. April 10, 2017. https://www.lincoln.edu/news-and-events/news/lincoln-university-unveils-historic-academic-partnership-barnes-foundation

27. Glueck, Grace. "Small University Gains Control of the Barnes Foundation." *New York Times*. October 19, 1989. https://www.nytimes.com/1989/10/19/arts/small-university-gains-control-of-the-barnes-foundation.html

28. Fleeson, Lucinda. "Lincoln U to Control $1 Billion Barnes Art Collection." *Philadelphia Inquirer*. September 27, 1988. https://www.inquirer.com/philly/entertainment/Lincoln_U_to_control_1_Billion_Barnes_art_collection.html

29. "Allocations for Lincoln U." Barnes Foundation. Accessed December 27, 2020. http://www.barnesfriends.org/downlload/Allocations%20for%20Lincoln%20in%20HB%201634%20(2003-04).pdf

30. Nietzel, Michael T. "Six HBCUs Receive Gifts Totaling More Than $100 Million from MacKenzie Scott." *Forbes*. July 29, 2020. https://www.forbes.com/sites/michaeltnietzel/2020/07/29/six-hbcus-receive-gifts-totaling-more-than-100-million-from-mackenzie-scott/?sh=3e7d32cc646b

31. "Hedge Fund Investor, Wife Donate $10M to Spelman College." AP News. August 19, 2020. https://apnews.com/article/atlanta-scholarships-reed-hastings-7c540a387a7d76a133e97cc81400459e

32. Stirgus, Eric. "Couple Starts $1 Million Scholarship Fund for Spelman College Students." *Atlanta Journal-Constitution*. June 2, 2020. https://www.ajc.com/news/local-education/couple-starts-million-scholarship-fund-for-spelman-college-students/gmjtfHpyeuJhO7cwj9FEpO/

33. de la Merced, Michael, and Andrew Ross Sorkin. "Bloomberg to give $100 Million to Black Medical Schools." *New York Times*. September 3, 2020. https://www.nytimes.com/2020/09/03/business/dealbook/bloomberg-black-medical-schools-donation.html#:~:text=Bloomberg%2C%20the%20billionaire%20and%20former,up%20to%20%24100%2C000%20in%20grants.

34. "Oprah Winfrey Announces $13 Million Gift to Morehouse College for Scholars Fund." Morehouse College. October 7, 2019. https://inside.morehouse.edu/news/news-inside/oprah-winfrey-announces-13-million-gift-to-morehouse-college-for-scholars-fund.html

35. Carter, Kelley, and Randall Williams. "Oprah Winfrey Donates $2 Million to HBCU Tennessee State and Its Surrounding Community." The Undefeated.

May 20, 2020. https://theundefeated.com/features/oprah-winfrey-donates-2-million-to-hbcu-tennessee-state-and-its-surrounding-community/

36. Douglas-Gabriel, Danielle. "Robert F. Smith's Morehouse Pledge Is Getting a Lot Bigger." *Washington Post.* September 20, 2019. https://www.washington post.com/local/education/robert-f-smiths-morehouse-pledge-is-getting-a-lot-bigger/2019/09/20/1ab08e6e-ce6f-11e9-b29b-a528dc82154a_story.html

37. Alexander, Sophie. "Billionaire Created a Perfect Experiment by Erasing $34 Million in Student Debt." *Bloomberg.* July 24, 2020. https://www.bloombergquint.com/business/a-34-million-student-debt-wipe-out-sets-up-a-perfect-economic-experiment

38. "Dominion Energy Commits $35 Million for HBCUs, Minority Students." *Philanthropy News Digest.* July 20, 2020. http://philanthropynewsdigest.org/news/dominion-energy-commits-35-million-for-hbcus-minority-students

39. "LeMoyne-Owen College Receives $40 Million Endowment, Largest in School's History." LeMoyne-Owen College News Release. July 2, 2020. https://www.localmemphis.com/article/news/education/lemoyne-owen-college-receives-40-million-endowment/522-48e4bdc9-2b92-4603-86fb-ffde9756d926#:~:text=MEMPHIS%2C%20Tenn%20%E2%80%94%20LeMoyne%2DOwen,in%20its%20158%2Dyear%20history.

40. "Augusta National Creates Golf Scholarships at Paine College Honoring Lee Elder." HBCU Sports. November 9, 2020. https://www.hbcusports.com/2020/11/09/augusta-national-creates-golf-scholarships-at-paine-college-honoring-lee-elder/

41. Milligan, Rashad. "Phil Mickelson Donates $500k to Jackson State, Possibly More to Come." *USA Today.* November 24, 2020. https://golfweek.usatoday.com/2020/11/24/phil-mickelson-donates-500k-to-jackson-state-possibly-more-to-come/

42. Chiari, Mike. "Capital One's The Match Donating Total of $4.4 Million to HBCU." Bleacher Report. November 27, 2020. https://bleacherreport.com/articles/2919951-capital-ones-the-match-donating-total-of-44-million-to-hbcus

43. Kyaw, Arrman. "NBA Legend Charles Barkley Pledges $1 Million to Tuskegee University." Diverse Education. November 3, 2020. https://diverseeducation.com/article/195338/

44. "A List of All HBCUs." HBCU Radio Net. Accessed December 27, 2020. http://hbcuradionet.whur.com/hbcu-list/

45. Harris, Adam. "Why America Needs Its HBCUs." *Atlantic.* May 16, 2019. https://www.theatlantic.com/education/archive/2019/05/howard-universitys-president-why-america-needs-hbcus/589582/

46. "Rosenwald Schools." National Trust for Historic Preservation. Accessed December 27, 2020. https://savingplaces.org/places/rosenwald-schools#.X7BGeVNKhTY

CHAPTER FOUR

Deposit Money into Black-Owned Banks

I am asking you to deposit at least 8.46% of your bank savings in Black-owned banks and leave it there for at least three years. Up to $250,000 will be fully guaranteed by the FDIC. Therefore, just as when you use a white bank, NO RISK!

"The banking system can create money through the process of making loans."[1]

THE ABSENCE OF banks in the Black community is akin to the canary in the coal mine. The death of the canary signifies that there is human danger due to a lack of oxygen in the area. Black communities without banks are also starved of metaphorical oxygen in the mines of financial resources needed for people to live healthy lives. The primary role of a bank is to lend money, which helps individuals improve their quality of life. The money is used to buy homes, pay for education, and finance businesses. Most communities bereft of this wonderful financial machine are private enterprise deserts, and such communities are not healthy because they lack a low-cost financial services ecosystem.

In contrast, one of the indicators of a healthy, thriving community is the presence of banks with the ability to lend a far greater amount of money to residents than was deposited. This phenomenon is called the "money multiplier" and works in the following way:

1. Martin deposits $100 in Chase Bank.
2. Chase engages in "Fractional Reserve Lending," whereby they hold $10 in reserves and lend $90 to Rosa.
3. Rosa uses $90 to buy a house from Malcolm.
4. Malcolm takes the $90 and deposits it into his account at Bank of America.
5. Bank of America holds $9 in reserve and lends Ida $81.
6. Ida pays W.E.B. $81 for a house.
7. W.E.B. deposits $81 in his account at Wells Fargo Bank.

Thus, from Martin's initial $100, a sum of $271 ($100 + $90 + $81) is now deposited in three banks. Money was created, as if by magic!

Unfortunately, this wonderful phenomenon of creating money is mostly impossible for Black banks, which hurts the Black community because there are fewer dollars to lend. The primary source of the problem stems from the fact that Black banks rely on deposits from the Black community, which, as this book has repeatedly stated, is poverty stricken. The Stanford Center on Poverty and Inequality released a report in 2017 that showed the trends in poverty rates by race/ethnicity in the U.S. from 1980 to 2015. As a singular group, the poverty level for

Black people has been almost two times that of Whites and has widened further since the Great Recession.[2]

Obviously, Black banks need resources from people other than the Black community. The bank deposits from people who are financially challenged are typically smaller and do not remain in the bank very long because the money is needed for everyday living. Looking at these elements more closely reveals the depth of the problem facing Black banks and, by extension, the Black community.

The official poverty level for a household of three people is $21,330 of annual income.[3] Using my old community of Englewood in Chicago as an example, there are approximately 75,000 residents and an average household income of $25,000. If we assume an annual rent of 35% of annual gross income, that would be $8,750, and if we assume total federal and state taxes of 20%, that would be $5,000. These two deductions would total $13,750, leaving $11,250 for a family of three to be fed, clothed, and provided for generally. While this example might seem extreme, data supports the thesis regarding this dire situation. The average deposit by a White person is 75% greater than that of a Black person. Therefore, when a Black person is able to deposit money into a savings account, it is likely to be something small and subject to frequent withdrawals. Black banks need larger deposits that remain in accounts for multiple years. This need is supported by William Michael Cunningham, an economist and banking expert who said, "Without assets and scale, Black banks are limited in the amount of lending they can do. No lending means no significant economic development."[4]

Therefore, in the words of a Black banker, **"The best way to support Black wealth creation is simple: bank Black! Even if you are White."** And I completely agree.

Black-Owned Banks versus White-Owned Banks

Disappointingly, White-owned banks, including Chase, Bank of America, and Wells Fargo, have a long history, continuing into the present, of not providing loans to Black people. This anti-Black financial discrimination has been going on for over a century. In 1921, a White bank employee told the following story about his bank's lending practice, "Negroes are usually allowed $1,000 to the white man's $1,500; only 35 per cent of the value of the property is loaned to the Negro, whereas 50 per cent is granted to whites. Maximum time of loan was five years for the White and three years for the Negro."[5] Ironically, this practice of Blacks being given only a portion of what was given to Whites dates back to the Constitution, which gave Blacks only three fifths the human recognition as Whites. In contrast, Black-owned banks, despite their small numbers and assets, have been tremendously supportive of the Black community.

In fact, there is a direct relationship between the actions of Black-owned banks and the growth of Black businesses. From 1888 to 1934, the number of Black businesses grew from 4,000 to 50,000.[6] During this period, Blacks owned more than 130 Black banks. Their support of Black entrepreneurs had positive impacts on the Black community in several ways: jobs were created; products and services were provided; and many of these entrepreneurs used their resources to support civil rights activism.

Arthur George "A.G." Gaston was an extraordinarily successful Black entrepreneur. His wealth – which exceeded $100 million – came from real estate investments. The first land that he purchased was financed by a $200 loan from a Black bank.[7] He built and developed the A.G. Gaston Motel, which was a regular meeting place in Birmingham, Alabama, during the Civil Rights Movement in the 1960s. When Dr. King was arrested in Birmingham, Gaston paid the $160,000 bond for Dr. King's release.[8]

Another positive aspect of Black banks is their reputation for treating customers as not just depositors but more like family members. When Hurricane Katrin hit Louisiana in 2005, it caused over $100 billion of damage in New Orleans. Many residents' homes were flooded, and they thus lost all of their assets. Liberty Bank, Black owned, allowed customers to withdraw as much as $500 from ATMs despite not knowing if those customers had sufficient deposits to cover the transaction. The bank lost only $1 from that kind act of humanity. The bank president, Alden McDonald Jr., told the *New York Times*, "Some say a banker is someone who gives you an umbrella when the sun is shining and takes it away when it starts to rain. We try not to be that banker."[9]

That mantra has been a consistent theme uttered by Black-owned banks for over a century. And the importance of Black-owned banks has not waned. When you look at Black bank lending over time, you can see that during the economic crisis, Black banks answered the call. Amid the weak housing market, from 2007 to 2013, the number of mortgages originated by Black-owned banks for Black borrowers rose 57% (from 1,035 to 1,624), despite a 36% decline in the number of Black-owned banks (from 48 to 28) and a 69% drop in all mortgage lending to Black borrowers.[10] And, since the Great Recession, Black banks have continued to loan in greater shares to people in low- and moderate-income census tracts, most of whom are Black.

Black banks have not only helped the Black community by providing mortgages, but they also did not hurt the Black community with bad mortgages. During the housing collapse a decade ago, not one Black bank issued a subprime mortgage. However, that was not true of White-owned banks. "They sent subprime lenders to Black communities and not to others, to sell subprime loans. The resulting impact was devastating. Blacks lost 53% of their wealth."[11]

Black banks again answered the call for the Black community in 2020 when the government made $670 billion available as low- and no-interest-rate loans that could be converted into grants. This program, the Payroll Protection Plan, was an unprecedented method of providing relief capital to small businesses during the coronavirus pandemic, primarily through large White banks. The center responsible for lending estimated correctly that "as many as 95% of Black businesses stood no chance of securing a PPP loan."[12] Research by the National Community Reinvestment Coalition found that "Black business owners with a comparable profile as White ones were less likely to be told that they met the qualifications needed for a PPP loan."[13] But Black-owned banks and those that are Black led and target lending to the Black community did what White banks declined to do. They provided PPP funding to Black-owned businesses. One of those banks was Seaway National Bank in Chicago, which at one time was the largest Black-owned bank in the country. The bank's president, Daryl Newell, reported in my podcast "Yay! Black Businesses Got PPP Money!" that 50% of the PPP funding recipients were Black-owned businesses. The bank sent 63% of its total PPP dollars to that 50%.

Mortgages

The positive story about Black banks includes individuals as well as businesses. Of the mortgages issued by Black-owned banks, 70% has gone to Black people, compared to less than 1% of mortgages issued by White-owned banks going to Black people.[14] One reason for this disparity can be explained simply by the revelation in the 2020 Home Mortgage Disclosure Act indicating that banks denied Black applicants for mortgages at a rate of 80% higher than white applicants.[15] Indeed, I was one of those Blacks who was rejected for a mortgage by a White bank.

In 1988, after owning two homes in Indiana and North Carolina for the previous seven years, my family and I moved to Chicago. My ex-wife and I had impeccable credit and secure employment. We had never been late with a mortgage payment. When we applied for a mortgage with Citicorp Mortgage Inc. to buy our new home, I was confident that approval was a certainty given our income, credit scores, and mortgage history. To my surprise, I was informed that our mortgage application was being rejected. I immediately asked him to check to ensure that my application was not being mixed up with someone else's. He assured me there was no mistake. I asked to meet with the branch manager and told him that I was surprised and disappointed with their decision. Then I told him that my belief was that my application was rejected because I was Black. I told him that if I did not qualify for a mortgage, then nobody should be able to qualify. He listened and asked if he could have a day to review everything. A few hours later, he called to tell me the mortgage had been approved.

Although I acquired the mortgage with Citicorp, I did not view it as a big victory. The reason I did not celebrate this individual victory was because my getting a mortgage after being rejected was not a triumph against systematic anti-Black discrimination. I had the same feelings at the end of the movie *12 Years a Slave*. Solomon, a free Black man who had been illegally enslaved, was freed after a dozen years of bondage. While I was happy for him as an individual, I did not view his singular emancipation as a great victory because there were still millions of Black people enslaved. The systemic, anti-Black institution of American slavery did not suffer from Solomon's lone release, the same way that the institutionalized discrimination against Blacks by financial organizations was not affected by overturning the rejection of my mortgage application.

Contract Selling

My displeasure about what happened to me with Citicorp led me to refinance my mortgage with Sears Mortgage Corporation, a division of the Sears department stores. But this discriminatory behavior from banking institutions is embedded in our country's history.

In 1952, my grandparents were denied a mortgage from a bank because they were Black. They had an impeccable credit rating, and my grandfather had steady employment throughout the previous decade at a steel mill outside of Gary, Indiana. After being rejected for a traditional mortgage, my grandparents acquired the home from the White seller under what was known as contract selling. This type of contract today is known as "seller financing." The home's owner finances the purchase through debt payments from the buyer. As the *Chicago Reader* newspaper reported, contract selling flourished during this period as the alternative to mortgages for Blacks. By one estimate, 85% of the homes purchased by Black Chicagoans in the 1950s were acquired through contracts rather than traditional bank mortgages.[16] These contracts had higher purchase prices and higher interest rates. Over the course of a contract, a buyer could pay upwards of 35 times more for a house than the seller paid to acquire it. In the documentary "The Color Tax: Origins of the Modern Day Racial Wealth Gap," as well as research from Duke University's Samuel DuBois Cook Center on Social Equity, reported that Blacks who had contract deals paid on average $71,000 more for their homes than they would have paid with FHA guaranteed mortgages from a bank.[17]

Even more startling is that the seller retained the deed and the buyer could be evicted without a return of the down payment. A study by Duke University titled "The Plunder of Black Wealth in Chicago"[18] concluded the following:

1. Between 75% and 95% of homes sold to Black families during the 1950s and 1960s were sold via contract.
2. Blacks who purchased on contract, on average, paid an additional $587 (in current dollars) more per month compared with what they would have under a conventional mortgage.[19]

My grandparents James and Augusta Grant escaped their predatory contract on June 16, 1956, when they purchased their home with a mortgage from the same Sears company that I used 33 years later!

This mistreatment of Blacks by White banks persists today. In 2012, Wells Fargo was sued, and agreed to a settlement of $175 million for charging higher fees and interest rates to Black customers, compared to White customers with similar credit profiles. A year later, Bank of America was fined for racial discrimination in lending practices.

Financial Apartheid

Currently, there are only 21 Black-owned banks, and they are relatively small. Collectively, these banks have less than $6 billion in assets.[20] The four largest White-owned banks have over $15 trillion, which is nearly 45% of the industry's total assets.[21] We need these banks to lend more of their trillions to the Black community. At the same time, we need more Black-owned banks and, for those in business today, we need to grow their deposit levels so that they have more money to lend.

Black-owned banks, like HBCUs, were not founded with the objective of competing against White-owned institutions. As we teach students at HBS, both were created to "satisfy unmet customer demand," which is the foundation of innovation. Thus, the innovative spirit of Black entrepreneurs was unleashed to serve the Black community, filling the spaces left by the anti-Black practices and discriminatory policies of Whites. Many White banks would gladly take deposits from Black customers but would rarely provide lending services to those same customers. Without that service, Black wealth opportunities were diminished or completely voided because, unlike the situations for White bank patrons, Black bank patrons could not get money for home mortgages, business loans, or education loans, all of which are required for wealth creation.

A perfect example of this financial apartheid was practiced in New York, where it was not an anomaly but prevalent throughout the country. The Chelsea Bank, a White-owned bank in the early 1920s, had deposit assets that came almost entirely from Black Harlem residents. Virtually no loans were given to Black customers. Instead, as one White employee of the bank reported, "All of this money is transferred downtown to the home office where it is loaned to White customers."[22] I have coined this practice "Black money, White wealth."

Freedman's Bank

Unfortunately, this abusive treatment of Blacks by banks did not begin in the 1920s, but almost a half century earlier in 1865 with the creation of the Freedman's Bank. This was the first bank ever created by the federal government, and it happened the same year that the 13th Amendment was passed to abolish slavery.

As Mehrsa Baradaran, an expert on the history of Black banks, has said, instead of giving Black people land confiscated from the Confederate soldiers found guilty of treason, the government gave them a bank with no money in it. While their desire for land in order to farm and build their own homes was a top priority for the former enslaved, many Whites felt that Blacks did not deserve reparations of any kind, including and especially land. This was stated clearly when the new president of Freedman's Bank said, "Their notion of having land given to them by the government is passing away, and we hear them saying 'We will work and save and buy for themselves.'"[23]

Freedman's Savings was a bank designed to service Black people, but let's be clear: it was not owned by Black people. The board of 50 trustees and the president of Freedman's were all White. With an original mandate to operate strictly as a savings institution, by 1871 Freedman's had grown to include 37 branches in 17 states and the District of Columbia. In its 9-year history, Freedman's received more than $57 million in deposits, serving almost 70,000 depositors.[24] This $57 million would be valued at over $1 billion today and would make Freedman's the largest Black-owned bank in 2021. The target customer of Freedman's was the Black military veteran along with the four million former enslaved people.

When comparing a group of Freedman's bank account holders with a similarly situated group who did not have accounts, researchers found that the Freedman's customers were generally wealthier and better educated.[25] Although the research by Stein and Yannelis in 2019 showed an impressive profile of some of Freedman's customers, their success cannot be attributed solely to the act of depositing their money into Freedman's. There is no direct cause and effect because the bank did not loan money to its depositors. Instead, as with Chelsea Bank, Freedman's took Black deposits and invested the money in White people.

All of the potential that those Black deposits represented for its Black customers came to a screeching halt due to gross mismanagement of the Freedman's Bank. Its trustees deviated from the original charter advising conservative conduct to invest in government bonds, and started to behave like an investment banking firm, investing in risky railroad ventures and real estate speculation, and issuing unsecured loans to family members. While the bank was under financial duress, Freedman's trustees made an agreement with First National Bank, owned by Jay Cooke, brother to the president of Freedman's. First National Bank would offload their liabilities onto Freedman's balance sheet with no objection from Freedman's trustees. Many of these trustees and bank managers operated like thieves. As one White observer explained, the White managers entrusted with guarding the savings of the freed slaves looted the bank.[26] In February 1874, with barely a pulse left in Freedman's, Fredrick Douglass took over as president, but it was too late. The bank was closed in June 1874.[27] Afterwards, Douglass stated that the collapse of the bank "was equivalent to adding another 10 years of slavery to the Negro man."[28] It was not until 1888 that an actual Black-owned bank was chartered.[29]

Even more disturbing were the real economic consequences radiating from the bank's demise. More than 60,000 depositors suffered nearly $3 million in losses. Federal deposit insurance did not exist as it does now, so it took arduous legal fights for some of the depositors to reclaim 62 cents for every dollar of their deposits. However, many never received a penny. This was another example of Black wealth destruction as a result of White behavior. This story is a concrete illustration of why many in the Black community struggle to trust White institutions. In response to their distrust, the Black community decided to create its own banks. The cause and effect of this narrative was best captured and commented on by Black scholar W.E.B. DuBois when he said, "Of all disgraceful swindles perpetrated on a struggling people, the Freedmen's Bank was among the worst, and the Negro did well not to wait for justice but went to banking himself as soon as his ignorance and poverty allowed."[30] Two University of Chicago professors reached the same conclusion in 2020, stating, "Freedman's collapse lead to Black mistrust of financial institutions."[31]

Maggie L. Walker

Black ownership of banks reached its zenith in the 1920s when there were 130 Black banks. One of those pioneers was Maggie L. Walker, the daughter of an enslaved woman, who, in 1903, became the first Black women to start a bank, St. Luke's Penny Savings in Richmond, Virginia. Maggie L. Walker's bank initiative began with her famous quote: "Let us put our moneys together; let us use our moneys; let us put our money out at usury among ourselves and reap the benefit ourselves. Let us have a bank that will take the nickels and turn them into dollars."[32] When the bank opened on November 2, 1903, over 280 customers opened new accounts, including one person who deposited 31 cents. By 1924, the bank had 50,000 depositors. By 1920, the bank had helped Black people buy 600 homes. The impact of this bank on the Black community was not limited to Richmond, Virginia, but had a national influence. For example, St. Luke's provided mortgages to Black entrepreneurs in New York City to buy apartment complexes in uptown Manhattan. At the time, there were no Black banks in New York.

Maggie Walker personified Black brilliance. She was more than a banker. She was an American hero, an unabashed "race woman." She proclaimed, "God knows I love this race of mine, especially the women."[33] This bank had several women on its board of trustees. A year after founding the bank, Walker opened the St. Luke Emporium, a department store that provided jobs for Black women and an opportunity to shop alongside White-owned stores. The targeted customer base for this store was the Black community of Richmond, Virginia. At the time, Black people could only enter and exit the White-owned department stores through a side or back door. Unlike White patrons, Black customers were not permitted to try on clothes before purchasing them. St. Luke Emporium eliminated those indignities for its Black patrons, providing jobs and affordable goods. She also owned the *St. Luke Herald,* a newspaper targeting Black readers that had 4,000 subscribers. The Black entrepreneurship and capitalism that Maggie Walker practiced followed a formula of not financially supporting businesses with anti-Black philosophies and practices. She boldly stated, "The only way we can kill the lion of race prejudice is to stop feeding them."[34] This genius of a businesswoman was committed to helping the Black community in as many ways as possible. In 1932, she started the first Girl Scouts troop in the country that had Black members.

When she died in 1934, the city and state flags flew at half-mast. Other honors include the Maggie L. Walker School, a middle school in Brooklyn, New York, as well as the Maggie L. Walker Governor's School for Government and International Studies, a high school in her hometown of Richmond, Virginia. Her home, which she purchased for $4,800 in 1904, originally had 5 rooms. She continued to add rooms for her sons and their families. Today, the 28-room home, located in the Jackson Ward community, known as the "Harlem of the South" because it was a prosperous Black business corridor, is a registered National Historic Site landmark with over 9,000 visitors touring the house each year.[35] The significance of this woman with her giant accomplishments benefitting the Black community is memorialized with a 10-foot statue of her standing in the Maggie L. Walker Memorial Plaza. Finally, in recognition for her pitch for Black self-reliance through Black banking, Kansas City's Federal Reserve Bank published a book in 2019 with her famous words as part of the title: *Let Us Put Our Money Together: The Founding of America's First Black Banks.*[36]

Banking Black

The "call to action" to help the Black community through Black banking has resonated with many companies. In 2020, *Fortune* magazine called this the Fortune 500 trend to "Bank Black." Netflix announced it would deposit $100 million, 2% of its total cash, into Black-owned banks and financial institutions.[37] Costco announced it would put $25 million into the Netflix-seeded Black Economic Development Fund.[38] Created by the Local Initiative Support Corporation (LISC), a Black-led community development financial institution, the fund will allocate the money to Black-owned banks. Biogen, a Boston-based biotech company, is depositing $10 million of its capital into America's largest Black-owned bank, OneUnited.[39] PayPal also pledged as much as $400 million to banks focused on the Black community. PayPal made good on that pledge by transferring $50 million to Optus Bank, a Black-owned bank in South Carolina.[40] That deposit helped Optus's assets swell 67% during the coronavirus pandemic to $150 million.

Before 2020 ended, the following headline was announced about a team in the National Basketball Association: "Hawks Announce Historic Agreement with Black-Owned Banks." This new transaction was a loan of $35 million being provided to the Atlanta Hawks by a consortium of eight Black banks. The profits from this loan will improve the bank's capital equity ratio, allowing them to increase the deposits they can receive from customers. Robert James reinforced the significance of this deal when he said, "What we earn from this loan strengthens our collective ability to provide even more loans and financial services to Black small businesses and consumers."[41]

How to Make Deposits

Table 4.1 presents a listing of Black-owned banks. The needs of Black banks center on capital infusions that generate assets and provide the banks with scale. The Netflix and PayPal examples offer some benchmarks about the types of capital that businesses have provided. Therefore, the best way to support Black wealth creation is simple: Bank Black! Even if you are White.

Companies

1. Using the list of Black banks in Table 4.1, locate a bank in your state, if one exists.
2. Open a business account with that bank, preferably equivalent to at least 8.46% of your cash balance.
3. Open a business line of credit with the bank.

Individuals

1. Using the list of Black banks in Table 4.1, locate a bank in your state, if one exists.
2. Open a savings account with that bank, preferably equivalent to at least 8.46% of your cash balance.
3. Establish an investing, retirement, wealth management relationship with that bank.

Table 4.1   Black-owned banks, state-by-state breakdown[42]

Alabama

OneUnited Bank: Multiple ATM locations

Alamerica Bank: Birmingham

Citizens Trust Bank: Birmingham and Eutaw

Commonwealth National Bank: Mobile

Liberty Bank: Montgomery and Tuskegee

Metro Bank: Ashville, Heflin, Lincoln, Moody, Pell City, Ragland, and Southside

Hope Credit Union: Montgomery

Alaska

OneUnited Bank: Multiple ATM locations

Arizona

OneUnited Bank: Multiple ATM locations

Arkansas

OneUnited Bank: Multiple ATM locations

Hope Credit Union: College Station, Little Rock, Pine Bluff, and West Memphis

California

OneUnited Bank: Multiple ATM locations, in addition to corporate office and Crenshaw branch, as well as upcoming Compton branch

Broadway Federal Bank: Los Angeles

(Continued)

Table 4.1   (Continued)

Colorado

OneUnited Bank: Multiple ATM locations

Connecticut

OneUnited Bank: Multiple ATM locations

Delaware

OneUnited Bank: Multiple ATM locations

District of Columbia

Industrial Bank: District of Columbia (Anacostia Gateway Banking Center, Ben's Chili Bowl, DC Court of Appeals, DC Superior Court, F Street Banking Center, Forestville Banking Center, Georgia Avenue Banking Center, J.H. Mitchell Banking Center, Nationals Park, Oxon Hill Banking Center, and U Street Banking Center

Howard University Employees Federal Credit Union: C B Powell Building

Florida

OneUnited Bank: Multiple ATM locations, in addition to Miami branch

FAMU Federal Credit Union: Tallahassee

Georgia

OneUnited Bank: Multiple ATM locations

Carver State Bank: Savannah

Citizens Trust Bank: Atlanta, Decatur, East Point, Lithonia, Stone Mountain, and Stonecrest

Table 4.1 (Continued)

Unity National Bank: Atlanta

1st Choice Credit Union: Atlanta

Credit Union of Atlanta: Atlanta

Omega Psi Phi Fraternity Federal Credit Union: Toccoa

Hawaii

OneUnited Bank: Multiple ATM locations

Idaho

OneUnited Bank: Multiple ATM locations

Illinois

OneUnited Bank: Multiple ATM locations

GN Bank: Chicago

Liberty Bank: Forest Park

South Side Community Federal Credit Union: Chicago

Indiana

OneUnited Bank: Multiple ATM locations

Iowa

OneUnited Bank: Multiple ATM locations

First Security Bank: Aredale, Charles City, Dumont, Hampton, Ionia, Manly, Marble Rock, Nora Springs, Riceville, Rockford, Rockwell, Rudd, and Thornton

(Continued)

Table 4.1   (Continued)

Kansas

OneUnited Bank: Multiple ATM locations

Liberty Bank: Kansas City

Kentucky

OneUnited Bank: Multiple ATM locations

Liberty Bank: Louisville

Louisiana

OneUnited Bank: Multiple ATM locations

Liberty Bank: Baton Rouge and New Orleans

Hope Credit Union: New Orleans

Southern Teachers & Parents Federal Credit Union: Baton Rouge, and Thibodaux

Maine

OneUnited Bank: Multiple ATM locations

Maryland

OneUnited Bank: Multiple ATM locations

The Harbor Bank of Maryland: Baltimore, Randallstown, and Silver Spring

Massachusetts

OneUnited Bank: Multiple ATM locations, in addition to corporate headquarters and Roxbury branch

Table 4.1 (Continued)

Michigan

OneUnited Bank: Multiple ATM locations

First Independence Bank: Clinton Township, and Detroit

Liberty Bank: Detroit

Minnesota

OneUnited Bank: Multiple ATM locations

Mississippi

OneUnited Bank: Multiple ATM locations

Liberty Bank: Jackson

Hope Credit Union: Biloxi, Drew, Greenville, Jackson, Louisville, Macon, Moorhead, Robinsonville, Shaw, Terry, Utica, and West Point

Missouri

OneUnited Bank: Multiple ATM locations

Liberty Bank: Kansas City

St. Louis Community Credit Union: Ferguson, Florissant, Pagedale, Richmond Heights, St. John, St. Louis, University City, and Wellston

Montana

OneUnited Bank: Multiple ATM locations

Nebraska

OneUnited Bank: Multiple ATM locations

(Continued)

Table 4.1   (Continued)

Nevada

OneUnited Bank: Multiple ATM locations

New Hampshire

OneUnited Bank: Multiple ATM locations

New Jersey

OneUnited Bank: Multiple ATM locations

Industrial Bank: Newark

New Mexico

OneUnited Bank: Multiple ATM locations

New York

OneUnited Bank: Multiple ATM locations

Carver Federal Savings Bank: Brooklyn, Jamaica, and Manhattan

Industrial Bank: New York City

Urban Upbound Federal Credit Union: Long Island City

North Carolina

OneUnited Bank: Multiple ATM locations

Mechanics & Farmers Bank: Charlotte, Durham, Greensboro, Raleigh, and Winston-Salem

First Legacy Community Credit Union: Charlotte

Greater Kinston Credit Union: Kinston

Table 4.1   (Continued)

North Dakota

OneUnited Bank: Multiple ATM locations

Ohio

OneUnited Bank: Multiple ATM locations

Faith Community United Credit Union: Cleveland

Toledo Urban Federal Credit Union: Toledo

Oklahoma

OneUnited Bank: Multiple ATM locations

Oregon

OneUnited Bank: Multiple ATM locations

Pennsylvania

OneUnited Bank: Multiple ATM locations

United Bank of Philadelphia: Philadelphia

Hill District Federal Credit Union: Pittsburgh

Rhode Island

OneUnited Bank: Multiple ATM locations

South Carolina

OneUnited Bank: Multiple ATM locations

OPTUS Bank: Columbia

Brookland Federal Credit Union: West Columbia

Community Owned Federal Credit Union: Charleston

(Continued)

Table 4.1   (Continued)

South Dakota

OneUnited Bank: Multiple ATM locations

Tennessee

OneUnited Bank: Multiple ATM locations

Citizens Bank: Memphis and Nashville

Tri-State Bank: Memphis

Hope Credit Union: Jackson and Memphis

Texas

OneUnited Bank: Multiple ATM locations

Unity National Bank: Houston and Missouri City

Faith Cooperative Credit Union: Dallas

Mount Olive Baptist Church Federal Credit Union: Dallas

Oak Cliff Christian Federal Credit Union: Dallas

Utah

OneUnited Bank: Multiple ATM locations

Vermont

OneUnited Bank: Multiple ATM locations

Virginia

OneUnited Bank: Multiple ATM locations

Virginia State University Federal Credit Union: South Chesterfield

Table 4.1   (Continued)

Washington

OneUnited Bank: Multiple ATM locations

West Virginia

OneUnited Bank: Multiple ATM locations

Wisconsin

OneUnited Bank: Multiple ATM locations

Columbia Savings & Loan: Milwaukee

Wyoming

OneUnited Bank: Multiple ATM locations

If you are still seeking options for involvement, I have the example of a project that I am actively participating in with fellow Harvard Business School alums. A group of us got together and agreed that the best way to achieve impactful and positive change was to provide capital to Black-owned businesses and banks. Partnering with Boston Private Bank and Trust, we created a new financial program called the Impact Banking Initiative. The program requires the participant to open a bank account and deposit cash. We were able to negotiate a competitive yield with a sweetener that the more HBS depositors there are, the higher the interest rate. The funds would then be earmarked by Boston Private for new lending to Black-owned businesses and banks. If you choose this option you still have FDIC protection, it is still run through your one Boston Private account, and the yields on your deposit will reflect the yields that the receiving Black-owned banks choose to pay.

I worked with three classmates on the creation of this program: Don Rice (who is Black) and Leslie Bottorff and Stephen Bodurtha (who are White). Prior to this project, the last time that I collaborated with them on any assignment was when we were students in 1983. Almost four decades later, we came together to put money into Black banks. We agreed that each of us would deposit at least $100,000 and asked our classmates to do the same. Now, I am asking that you join us and make similar deposits, or whatever you can afford. This money will ultimately go towards strengthening the Black community. We cannot wait until anti-Black systematic racism is eliminated by White banks. The Black community needs help now, and Black banks are the proven means to provide that help.

Notes

1. "How Banks Create Money." Lumen Learning. Accessed December 27, 2020. https://courses.lumenlearning.com/wm-macroeconomics/chapter/how-banks-create-money/#:~:text=It%20is%20not%20just%20that,the%20process%20of%20making%20loans.&text=At%20this%20stage%2C%20Singleton%20Bank,pay%20its%20depositors%20interest%20either

2. Burton, Linda, Marybeth Mattingly, Juan Pedroza, and Whitney Welsh. "The Poverty and Inequity Report." Stanford Center on Poverty and Inequality. 2017. https://inequality.stanford.edu/sites/default/files/Pathways_SOTU_2017_poverty.pdf

3. "2019 Poverty Guidelines." aspe.hhs.gov. Accessed January 18, 2021. https://aspe.hhs.gov/poverty-guidelines

4. McKinney, Jeffrey. "Looking Back at the History of America's Black Banks, Even as They Strive for Vitality." *Black Enterprise*. August 30, 2019. https://www.Blackenterprise.com/Black-banks-struggle/

5. Tillotson, Amanda. "Race, Risk and Real Estate: The Federal Housing Administration and Black Homeownership in the Post World War II Home Ownership State." *DePaul J. Soc. Just.* 8 (2014): 25. https://via.library.depaul.edu/cgi/viewcontent.cgi?article=1099&context=jsj

6. "Minority Banking Timeline: 1888 Capital Savings Bank." Accessed December 27, 2020. https://www.fedpartnership.gov/minority-banking-timeline/

capital-savings-bank#:~:text=Between%201888%20and%201934%2C%20
134,increased%20from%204%2C000%20to%2050%2C000.

7. Hoover, Gary. "Arthur G. Gaston: Entrepreneur Against All Odds."
Archbridge Institute. October 29, 2018. https://www.archbridgeinstitute.
org/2018/10/29/arthur-g-gaston-entrepreneur-against-all-odds/

8. "A.G. Gaston Motel." National Trust for Historic Preservation. Accessed
December 27, 2020. https://savingplaces.org/places/a-g-gaston-motel#.
X9PQc8tKhhE

9. Rivlin, Gary. "Why New Orleans's Black Residents Are Still Underwater
After Katrina." *New York Times*. August 18, 2015. https://www.nytimes.
com/2015/08/23/magazine/why-new-orleans-black-residents-are-still-under-
water-after-katrina.html

10. Neal, Michael and John Walsh. "The Potential and Limits of Black-Owned
Banks." Urban Institute. March 2020. https://www.urban.org/sites/default/
files/publication/101849/the20potential20and20limits20of20black-owned-
20banks.pdf

11. "Testimony of Mehrsa Baradaran before the United States House of Representatives Subcommittee on Consumer Protection and Financial Institutions." April 9, 2019. https://www.congress.gov/116/meeting/house/109303/
witnesses/HHRG-116-BA15-Wstate-BaradaranM-20190409-U2.pdf

12. "$349 Billion COVID-19 Small Business Program Short-Changes Businesses
of Color." *Chicago Defender*. April 25, 2020. https://chicagodefender.com/349-
billion-covid-19-small-business-program-short-changes-businesses-of-color/

13. Zhou, Li. "The Paycheck Protection Program Failed Many Black-Owned Businesses." Vox. October 5, 2020. https://www.vox.com/2020/10/5/21427881/
paycheck-protection-program-black-owned-businesses

14. Vanek Smith, Stacey, and Darius Rafieyan. "Why We Need Black-Owned
Banks." NPR. July 8, 2020. https://www.npr.org/transcripts/889141681

15. "Black Applicants Are Far More Likely to be Denied a Mortgage, Limiting
Opportunity to Live 'The American Dream.'" PR Newswire via Zillow. August
4, 2020. https://www.prnewswire.com/news-releases/Black-applicants-are-
far-more-likely-to-be-denied-a-mortgage-limiting-opportunity-to-live-the-
american-dream-301105432.html#:~:text=A%20Zillow%C2%AE%20
analysis%20of,applying%20for%20a%20conventional%20loan.

16. Burns, Rebecca. "The Infamous Practice of Contract Selling Is Back in Chicago." *Chicago Reader*. March 1, 2017. https://www.chicagoreader.com/chicago/
contract-selling-redlining-housing-discrimination/Content?oid=25705647

17. Chiarito, Bob. "The Plunder of Black Wealth in Chicago, Captured in Film."
Chicago Reporter. June 5, 2019. https://www.chicagoreporter.com/the-plunder-
of-black-wealth-in-chicago-captured-in-film/

18. "The Plunder of Black Wealth in Chicago." Samuel DuBois Cook Center on Social Equity at Duke University. Accessed December 27, 2020. https://socialequity.duke.edu/portfolio-item/the-plunder-of-black-wealth-in-chicago-new-findings-on-the-lasting-toll-of-predatory-housing-contracts/

19. Moore, Natalie. "Contract Buying Robbed Black Families in Chicago of Billions." NPR. May 30, 2019. https://www.npr.org/local/309/2019/05/30/728122642/contract-buying-robbed-black-families-in-chicago-of-billions

20. Vanek Smith, Stacey, and Darius Rafieyan. "Why We Need Black-Owned Banks." NPR. July 8, 2020. https://www.npr.org/transcripts/889141681

21. Cox, Jeff. "5 Biggest Banks Now Own Almost Half the Industry." CNBC. April 15, 2015. https://www.cnbc.com/2015/04/15/5-biggest-banks-now-own-almost-half-the-industry.html

22. Baradaran, Mehrsa. *The Color of Money: Black Banks and the Racial Wealth Gap.* Harvard University Press, 2017, p. 78.

23. Ibid, p. 23.

24. "Freedman's Savings and Trust Company (Freedman's Bank), 1865–1874." National Archives and Records Administration. Accessed December 27, 2020. https://www.archives.gov/files/research/african-americans/freedmens-bureau/freedmens-bank.pdf

25. Doris, Aine. "How Powerful Is Financial Inclusion?" *Chicago Booth Review.* August 10, 2020. https://review.chicagobooth.edu/economics/2020/article/how-powerful-financial-inclusion

26. Baradaran. *The Color of Money*, p. 20.

27. "The Freedman's Savings Bank: Good Intentions Were Not Enough: A Noble Experiment Goes Awry." Office of the Comptroller of the Currency. Accessed December 27, 2020. https://www.occ.treas.gov/about/who-we-are/history/1863-1865/1863-1865-freedmans-savings-bank.html#:~:text=In%20March%201874%2C%20Frederick%20Douglass,But%20it%20was%20too%20late.

28. Chatman, Angie. "Black Americans' Rocky Relationship with Banks Can Be Traced Back to an Institution That Promised Wealth But Collapsed After Just 9 Years." *Business Insider.* September 23, 2020. https://www.businessinsider.com/personal-finance/freedmans-bank-collapse-black-americans-wealth-2020-9

29. Bradley, Jonathan. "The True Reformers Bank." Black Past. December 29, 2010. https://www.Blackpast.org/african-american-history/true-reformers-bank-1888-1910/

30. Baradaran. *The Color of Money*, p. 32.

31. Yannelis, Constantine. "Why a 19th-Century Bank Failure Still Matters." *UChicago News*. September 11, 2020. https://news.uchicago.edu/story/why-19th-century-bank-failure-still-matters

32. Howell, Lyman. "Black History Month: Maggie L. Walker: The Importance of Business Ownership." Accessed December 27, 2020. https://www.entrenuity.com/news-archive/Black-history-month

33. Wade, Reggie. "Meet the Woman Who Opened a Bank in the Confederacy's Capital During Jim Crow." Yahoo! Finance. February 15, 2019. https://au.finance.yahoo.com/news/first-black-woman-banker-bank-155141647.html

34. Sullivan, Shawn. "Maggie Walker, Turn of the Century Titan of Finance." *USA Today*. February 22, 2016, last modified May 4, 2017. https://www.usa-today.com/story/news/nation-now/2016/02/22/maggie-walker-turn-century-titan-finance/78439610/

35. "Maggie L. Walker National Historic Site." National Park Service. Accessed December 27, 2020. https://www.nps.gov/museum/exhibits/maggie_walker/rooms/house_tour.html

36. "Let Us Put Our Money Together: The Founding of America's First Black Banks." Federal Reserve Bank of Kansas City. Accessed December 27, 2020. https://www.kansascityfed.org/publications/aboutthefed/letusputourmoneytogether

37. de la Merced, Michael. "Netflix Moves $100 Million in Deposits to Bolster Black Banks." *New York Times*. June 30, 2020. https://www.nytimes.com/2020/06/30/business/dealbook/netflix-100-million-black-lenders.html

38. Carlstedt, Catherine. "Costco Commits $25 Million to LISC's Black Economic Development Fund." Local Initiatives Support Corporation. August 28, 2020. https://www.lisc.org/our-stories/story/costco-commits-25-million-to-liscs-black-economic-development-fund/

39. Wieczner, Jen. "Biogen Moves $10 Million to Black-Owned OneUnited, Joining the Fortune 500 Trend to 'Bank Black.'" *Fortune*. September 3, 2020. https://fortune.com/2020/09/03/biogen-Black-bank-oneunited-netflix-pay-pal-costco/#:~:text=Moving%20money%20to%20Black%2Downed,the%20company%20said%20Thursday%20morning

40. Crosman, Penny. "Why PayPal Just Deposited $50 Million in a Small South Carolina Bank." American Banker. August 26, 2020. https://www.americanbanker.com/news/why-paypal-just-deposited-50-million-in-tiny-optus-bank#:~:text=PayPal%20has%20just%20deposited%20%2450,sound%2C%20it%20happened%20relatively%20quickly

41. "Hawks Announce Historic Agreement With Black-Owned Banks." NBA. December 10, 2020. https://www.nba.com/hawks/hawks-announce-historic-agreement-black-owned-banks#:~:text=The%20Hawks%20Become%20the%20First,of%20Emory%20Sports%20Medicine%20Complex.&text=Georgia%2Dbased%20Carver%20State%20Bank%20served%20as%20the%20syndicate's%20Lead%20Arranger

42. Williams, Ward. "Black-Owned Banks by State." Investopedia. July 21, 2020. https://www.investopedia.com/Black-owned-banks-by-state-5024944

CHAPTER FIVE

Support Black-Owned Businesses

I am asking you to spend at least 8.46% of your annual household and business budgets with Black-owned businesses.

"I think supporting Black-owned businesses is so important. Why? Everyone that works here, is from here. We are providing jobs in this community."[1]

The Importance of Black-Owned Businesses

Supporting Black business also means supporting Black communities because businesses are usually more than just places that offer goods and services.[2] Black entrepreneurs are the largest private employers of Black people in the country. When you support Black entrepreneurs, you are helping to close the Black-White wealth gap.

Two people who are likely to gain wealth as a result of public support of Black entrepreneurs are Sergio Hudson and

Christopher John Rogers. Both men own their own clothing design companies. Vice President Kamala Harris wore clothes they designed at the 2021 presidential inauguration.[3] This was a very intentional choice made by the vice president. As Paul Cobler, the reporter for the *Advocate*, wrote, "she made it a point to wear clothes by Black designers."[4] The positive financial impact on their companies was best explained the day after the inauguration by Alison Bringe, the chief marketing officer of an analytics company: "When Christopher John Rogers showed his spring collection at New York Fashion Week, the brand generated just over $1 million, while yesterday's events accumulated upward of 8 times that – in less than 24 hours."[5]

Black entrepreneurship not only enriches the company's owner but provides living wages to the employees. I travel the country giving speeches about Black entrepreneurs being my personal heroes and sheros because they create jobs. People with jobs are self-sufficient. And people who are self-sufficient tend to live in safer, healthier communities.

One indicator of a community's health is measured by the amount of money, in terms of spending, that remains in the community. In contrast, money that leaves a community is called "leakage." Leakage, in its simplest definition, is money a resident spends outside of the resident's neighborhood. In many cases, relevant goods and services are not available locally in Black communities. Based on analysis done by economists and economic development think tanks, a healthy community retains about 73 cents of every dollar.[6] These economic and demographic facts help identify the necessity and benefits of Black-owned businesses in Black communities, and why we need to grow them.

A great example of money not "leaking" out of the Black community is demonstrated in the actions of one Black owner of Brown Sugar Bakery in Chicago. The money she earns from sales gets put right back into the 75th Street Boardwalk's local economy. She buys her employees meals at Lem's BBQ across the street. Next door to Lem's is the dry cleaners she uses, and beside her bakery is a shop where she buys clothes.[7]

Black-owned businesses also help to make Black communities safer. *Chicago Tribune* columnist Clarence Page reported that Black men ages 18 to 24 will commit four times as many crimes as White men the same age, but when the research was controlled for the factor of employment, the difference virtually disappeared! These facts suggest that unemployment and poverty, not race, are most likely factors that underlie and create crime.

Therefore, the relevant question is "Who are the likely employers of young Black men and Blacks generally?" Resoundingly, the answer is Black entrepreneurs. If we look to strengthen Black communities, we need more Black-owned businesses. And, given their contributions to the economic, social, and cultural health of Black communities, Black businesses presently in operation need entrepreneurial and financial support to grow so that they can create more jobs. The simplest way for you to help Black businesses grow is to become a regular customer, buy their products, or use their services.

The employment practices of Black-owned businesses compared to White businesses, as it pertains to Black people, is striking and best highlighted in the research of Dr. Timothy Bates. In his book *Banking on Black Enterprise*, Bates uses a table to highlight employment practices that are quite revealing (see Table 5.1).

Bates's research clearly shows that the race of a business's owner matters as to who will be employed. Even White-owned companies in Black communities will employ far fewer Blacks than Black-owned companies located in White communities.

Table 5.1   Black employment practices

	Business owner	Location	Percentage of Black Employees
1.	Black-owned	Black community	85%
2.	White-owned	Black community	32%
3.	Black-owned	White community	75%
4.	White-owned	White community	15%

An example of this phenomenon occurred in a predominantly Black Austin community in Chicago. At one time, there were over 3,000 small White-owned manufacturing firms in that community employing 100,000 workers. However, although over 90% of the residents were Black, only 8% of those local Black residents were employed in those firms.

My personal observation of this employment practice happened last year during a visit to New Haven, Connecticut. I patronized a restaurant for breakfast in a predominantly Black community. The place was packed with only Black customers, but something seemed odd to me. None of the waitresses, waiters, cashiers, cooks, or busboys were Black; all were White. This reminded me of an episode of *Seinfeld* where the character Elaine noticed that all of the waitresses had similar body types. She complained to the male owner that he was discriminating against women with other body physiques. His response was, "These are all my daughters!" With this in mind, I asked to speak to the owner, who was a White man. The first thing I asked was, "Are all of the employees your relatives?" He responded, "No, why do you ask?" I then asked, "Do you have any Black employees who are not working today?" He answered, "No. And I see what you are asking! Please leave my restaurant now!"

In contrast, a predominantly White community that reflects an understanding of the productive relationship between Black business ownership and Black employment is Yellow Springs, Ohio. In December 2020, the city announced that it was selling the Miami Township Fire Station to comedian David Chappelle, who plans to convert the property into a 140-seat comedy club. Chappelle lives in the city. The city's press announcement included the following statement: "We think this will bring a new class of jobs to town. We also considered that [Chappelle] is a minority business owner, he has a history of employing minorities and he is a person who has a clear commitment to amplifying voices of color."[8]

Race in Business

The impact of race on the success of Black-owned businesses affects the marketing efforts of the owners when they choose to target non-Black customers. To avoid the challenges of race, many engage in a practice that I consider "racial concealment" where the Black entrepreneurs intentionally conceal their race. One of the country's greatest entrepreneurs, John Johnson, engaged in this practice when he sought to purchase a building on Michigan Avenue in downtown Chicago to house his successful magazine, *Ebony*. He inspected the building while accompanied by a White friend. Johnson dressed casually, like a janitor, while his friend wore a suit and tie, posing as the perspective buyer. Johnson believed that the White seller would never sell the building to a Black man, so he engaged in this ruse. Almost 50 years later, the same "racial concealment" was evident in the conduct of Robert Smith, a Black billionaire, when he chose not to place a photo of himself on his private equity funds website because he thought that if people knew he was Black they would not do business with his firm.[9]

Another Black entrepreneur, Duane Draughon, who owns a patio-installation company, shared his "racial concealment" practice: "I never said I wasn't the owner. If asked, I would admit it. But I always said I was either the project manager or a designer."[10] Draughon's clientele included White homeowners, but in his early efforts to grow his business, he encountered potential customers who slammed doors in his face or refused to allow him into their homes. After multiple such rejections, Draughon decided to erase all public information that a Black person owned his company. He even went as far as recruiting a White insurance company representative to conduct job interviews in assembling his White sales team.

One of the most interesting stories illustrating the intersection of race and business involves Sears, Roebuck and Company. Founded in 1887 as a mail order company, Sears was something like a predecessor of Amazon today: customers nationwide could buy just about anything from the Sears catalog. That was reflected in one of their jingles: "Sears has everything! They even sell homes!"[11] Perhaps even more important than products, Sears gave Black consumers the chance to avoid second-class treatment by White merchants. Typically, White merchants made Black customers enter and exit through the rear door, charged them higher prices, and sold them inferior food and products. With the introduction of Sears' mail order business, Blacks no longer had to go inside stores and could pay the same price for products as Whites because they were anonymous shoppers. They also could get the same quality of products.

As Sears became more and more successful, White business owners began to lose revenue from Black customers. As stated in a *Washington Post* article, by the turn of the century, some merchants were even encouraging people to bring in their catalogs for Sunday night bonfires, offering bounties of up to $50 for the person who brought the most Sears catalogs to the bonfire, as author Antonia Farzen reported. Local storekeepers even began circulating rumors that the company was owned by Black men.[12] This was done with the hope that White consumers would not shop at Sears. In response, the White founders of Sears published their photos in local newspapers.

More Than Employers

Supporting Black businesses results in benefits to the Black community beyond jobs and social health for its Black residents. In addition to creating jobs for Black people, Black entrepreneurs give back to the Black community in ways that have cultural and inspirational impact. Therefore, when you become a customer, you are also becoming a multipronged contributor to the Black community. Many are philanthropists, like Valerie Daniels-Carter, the founder of V & J Foods, the largest woman-owned franchisee in the country. She owns 137 total units consisting of Pizza Hut, Coffee Beanery, Burger King, Häagen-Dazs, and Auntie Anne's. She is part owner of the NBA's Milwaukee Bucks and the NFL's Green Bay Packers. However, what is most impressive is her philanthropy to Milwaukee's Black community. She donated money to build a community center in the heart of one of the city's most poverty-stricken communities. The center houses a Boys and Girls Club, a clinic that provides affordable healthcare, a credit union, and a business incubator for start-ups.[13]

Black in Print

Another great entrepreneur whose company helped the Black community was John H. Johnson, the founder of *Ebony* magazine. When he founded the magazine in 1945, there was an unwritten rule followed by most White-owned magazines and newspapers that the photo of a Black person would be published only if he or she had committed a crime. Mr. Johnson knew that this practice was detrimental to the perception of Black people by Whites and Blacks, so he created *Ebony* magazine to counter those negative images. He stated, "I created the magazine to tell the swell story about the American Negro." The absence of positive, unbiased stories about Blacks was not a figment of his imagination. This long-established, detrimental bias was finally acknowledged on December 20, 2020, in the headline of a prominent newspaper that stated, "The Truth in Black and White: An Apology from the Kansas City Star."[14] The opening paragraph read as follows:

> Today we are telling the story of a powerful local business that has done wrong.
>
> For 140 years, it has been one of the most influential forces in shaping Kansas City and the region. And yet for much of its early history – through sins of both commission and omission – it disenfranchised, ignored and scorned genera-tions of Black Kansas Citizens. It reinforced Jim Crow laws and redlining. Decade after early decade it robbed an entire community of opportunity, dignity, justice and recognition.
>
> That business is The Kansas City Star.

The article acknowledged "decades of coverage that depicted Black Kansas citizens as criminals living in a crime-laden world."

To counter this mistreatment, many Black entrepreneurs established newspapers, like HBCUs and Black banks, to service and support the Black community. One such newspaper was the *Chicago Defender*, which was the first Black newspaper to reach a circulation of 100,000 copies weekly. It achieved national cir-culation by 1917[15] and had an impact on Black communities throughout the nation. For example, it was instrumental in get-ting Blacks to leave the South en masse, to escape the blatant anti-Black, government-enforced policies and practices, including lynching. On September 2, 1916, its headline read, "The Exodus," with a photo of Black men, women, and children at a train station in Charleston, South Carolina.[16] The paper was successful in encouraging over six million Blacks to come to Northern cities, depleting the South of almost 50% of its Black population between 1910 and 1970.

As a consequence of the Great Migration, the White South was losing its cheap labor force, so they published false stories in local newspapers about Blacks freezing to death in Northern cities.[17] While the South was losing laborers, many of those Black men and women were coming to the North to work in Black-owned businesses. They were seeking to free themselves of racial injustices that were economic, political, and social. The idea of Black entrepreneurship being synonymous with the idea of Black freedom was not new, but it was growing.

A Brief History of Black Entrepreneurship in the United States

Black entrepreneurship began 32 years after the first Black slaves arrived in America. In 1651, Anthony Johnson, an ex-slave, purchased 250 acres of land in Virginia, becoming America's first Black property owner and entrepreneur.[18] Before the Emancipation Proclamation, before formal armed hostilities, free Blacks in the South and the North had an insatiable appetite for business ownership such that on the eve of the Civil War their collective wealth was conservatively estimated to be over $50 million.[19] Assuming a 4% interest rate over 150 years, that would amount to $15 billion in current day dollars.

Those early Black entrepreneurs include James Forten, who, in the late 1700s, owned a manufacturing company in

Philadelphia that made sails for ships. He employed more than 40 Black and White workers. In 1838, free Black women created jobs for themselves, and others, through their domination of the dressmaking and wig-making industries. In 1840, free Blacks in New York City also created jobs through their ownership of a clothes cleaner, a hairdressing salon, a confectionery, a fruit store, two coal yards, two dry goods stores, two restaurants, three tailor shops, and six boardinghouses.

Surprisingly, Black entrepreneurship was not limited to free Blacks. As an enslaved man in the early 1800s, Frank McWorter started a company that produced saltpeter, the main ingredient in gun powder.[20] With the company's profits, he purchased his freedom and the freedom of sixteen family members. Similarly, John Berry Meachum owned a carpentry business.[21] In addition to himself, Meachum purchased the freedom of his family and twenty friends. In 1794, Robert Renfro started a restaurant in Nashville, Tennessee, where he served food as well as liquor.[22] He purchased his freedom and a friend's freedom seven years later in 1801. Black people have used their entrepreneurship, literally, as a tool for freedom.

White Destruction of Black Businesses

As inspiring as these actions are to our modern sensibilities, they angered many White Americans at the time and, at different points in American history, became flashpoints for White mobs to commit anti-Black terrorist acts. Throughout history, Black entrepreneurial success has ignited some of the most vicious and violent anti-Black behavior of some Whites. If you go to the Legacy Museum in Montgomery, Alabama, you will see story after story chronicling instances of Black businesspeople being lynched, with mobs of Whites dressed in their Sunday best and bringing their children to attend the horrific "ceremony." As many as 4,000 Whites would gather to observe a lynching.[23] A searing example was the lynching of Thomas Moss, Calvin McDowell, and William Stewart. Their crime? They opened a grocery store in Memphis, Tennessee named "People's Grocery Company." Their store was across the street from a White-owned grocery store.[24]

But competing with White entrepreneurs was not the only crime that could result in Black entrepreneurs being killed. This was the experience of Anthony P. Crawford, a successful Black farmer who owned over 400 acres of land where he grew cotton. On October 21, 1916, Crawford took a wagonload of cotton to town in South Carolina. Newspaper accounts detailed:

> While waiting his turn at the gin that day, Crawford entered the mercantile store of W.D. Barksdale. Barksdale offered Crawford 85 cents a pound for his cottonseed. Crawford replied that he had a better offer. Barksdale called him a liar; Crawford called the storekeeper a cheat. Three clerks grabbed ax handles, and Crawford backed into the street, where the sheriff appeared and arrested Crawford – for cursing a white man. Released on bail, Crawford was cornered by about 50 whites who beat and knifed him. The sheriff carried him back to jail. A few hours later, a deputy gave the mob the keys to Crawford's cell. At sundown, they hanged him from a solitary Southern pine. No one was ever tried for the killing.[25]
>
> The Crawford land was purchased in 2000 by International Paper Corp. A company spokesman said International Paper was unaware of the land's history.

As I am writing this book, 2021 marks 100 years since the seminal incident of violence ever visited upon Blacks that was directly related to successful Black entrepreneurship, the well-known Tulsa race riot. As stated by John W. Rogers, Jr., great-grandson of J.B. Stradford and chairman of Ariel Capital Management, "Greenwood shows that when we are left to our own devices and don't have a knee to our neck, we can achieve extraordinary things. On the other hand, it shows you that unfortunately, so many times in our history when Black folks get a few steps ahead, we get pulled back down."[26]

In the "roaring twenties," one of the most affluent Black communities in America was not in New York or Chicago, but Tulsa, Oklahoma, also known as "Black Wall Street."[27] Fifteen thousand Blacks resided in the city and, in a 36-square-block area, they owned and operated over six hundred businesses.[28] A dollar would circulate 36 to 1,000 times, sometimes taking a year to leave the community. The main thoroughfare of this area was Greenwood Avenue, and, in this area, Black people owned 30 grocery stores, 21 restaurants, 6 private airplanes, 2 movie theaters, a hospital, a bank, and a bus system. There are Black communities today that are three times the size of Tulsa community back then that do not have this number or array of Black businesses.

Men like O.W. Gurley and J.B. Stradford saw growth opportunities and took full advantage. As the oil industry surged and Black people looked to leave the overly oppressive Jim Crow territories of the deep South, cities like Tulsa and its Greenwood section were beacons of light for a bright future. What was meant to be an exodus from the past was not to be, as Tulsa became another example of what happens when Black people have something that White people do not believe they should have. On June 21, 1921, in the blink of twelve hours, "Black Wall Street" was gone. An envious, angry, outraged mob of Whites burned down all of the businesses and killed 300 Black Americans in one of the most heinous acts in American history, a localized act of genocide. Those who survived were placed in internment centers for weeks or months. Greenwood's total property loss neared $2 million (over $50 million in current dollars). When I have given speeches about Tulsa, I have always ended the speech with the following sentence: "Most of the bodies have not been recovered and there are continuing efforts to bring dignity to the dead and closure for the descendants' families." In October 2020, an archaeological team unearthed a mass grave in Tulsa that could contain 30 coffins filled with the cadavers of Black Tulsans.[29]

Incidents like the Tulsa massacre were rampant two years earlier over the course of the "Red Summer" of 1919. That was a period where Black people were terrorized in more than three dozen cities across the United States in places like Chicago; Washington, D.C.; Elaine, Arkansas; Norfolk, Virginia; and Omaha, Nebraska. These cities had prosperous Black communities that lived in fear of reprisal from White people whose actions, in some instances, were sanctioned by the local government, like the Wilmington Insurrection of 1898.

What if I told you that a fairly large segment of the population did not like the legitimately elected, racially diverse government and decided to execute the only successful coup d'état in American history? Would you believe it actually happened? And, no, this was not a current event, but took place in 1898, in Wilmington, North Carolina. Similar to Tulsa, Wilmington was the home of a thriving Black community of roughly 55,000 people. The Black middle class was growing, and Black people served in a range of municipal government positions. Even in today's terms, Wilmington would be considered progressive in the biracial composition of its municipal government and especially so in that its Black people were able to dictate policy rather than feeling constrained to navigating a political labyrinth hoping not to upset their White counterparts. Black people also had significant economic power, with many former slaves applying their acquired skills profitably in the marketplace. At the time, Black people represented 10 to 30% of Wilmington's skilled craftsman. In addition, Blacks owned 10 of the city's 11 restaurants, were 90% of the city's 22 barbers, and operated one of the city's 4 fish and oyster dealerships.[30] There were also more Black bootmakers/shoemakers than White, one-third of the city's butchers were Black, as were one-half of the city's tailors. Despite all of that prosperity, there were still limitations on how much wealth Blacks could amass.

With the end of slavery, there was a lack of inherited wealth, limitations on access to credit, and the loss of savings stemming from the collapse of the Freedman's Bank that created an insurmountable situation in which Blacks "could not save anything" or otherwise acquire the means to own taxable property. The Black people of Wilmington made up 60% of the county's population but were only 8% of the property owners. The resulting disproportionately large tax burden on affluent Whites generated an anger and jealousy that fused with that of less affluent Whites in their resentment about any advancements of Black people. As time passed, resentment built up in the Whites of Wilmington and they formed their own coalition and overthrew the legally established government, leveraging a propaganda campaign igniting fear of local "Negro Rule":[31]

> North Carolina is a WHITE MAN'S STATE and WHITE MEN will rule it, and they will crush the party of Negro domination beneath a majority so overwhelming that no other party will ever dare to attempt to establish negro rule here. It will be the meanest, vilest, dirtiest campaign since 1876. The slogan of the Democratic party from the mountains to the sea will be but one word . . . Nigger![32]

White Wilmington citizens started organizing and forming White Supremacy Clubs (they literally called them White Supremacy Clubs), holding rallies and, ultimately, recruiting enough members to forcibly remove the government and terrorize as many Black people as they could. Estimates say that 60 to 300 Black people were killed, and at least 2000 were displaced, forced to abandon their businesses and properties. A change in government and the enforcement of Jim Crow laws and regulations that deprived Black people of equality developed as well. As for the treacherous White people who led the coup, several of them went on to become governors of North Carolina, and senators as well. If you ever need a demonstrative definition of White privilege, just look up what happened in Wilmington in 1898 and prepare to weep for our humanity.

Supporting Black-Owned Restaurants

My favorite Black-owned businesses are restaurants. I love them for multiple reasons. The most obvious is the delicious food. The communal atmosphere is always enjoyable too. At its best, when I am at a restaurant, I am reminded of large dining events filled with family, partaking of great food, and comforting conversations. In addition to its ambience and service, Black restaurants also make huge contributions to the Black community because they are great job creators, typically employing people from the community where they are located. While not mandatory, most Black-owned restaurants are located in Black communities. Therefore, they are contributing to the beautification and productivity of real estate in those communities.

As referenced above, not all Black-owned restaurants are located in Black communities. Yet I find that even those located in predominantly White communities, like Batters & Berries in the upscale Lincoln Park neighborhood of Chicago, still have primarily Black employees. My personal observation supports the research and findings of Dr. Timothy Bates. In his book *Banking on Black Enterprise*, he recognized that Black-owned businesses, despite their locations – whether in the city, suburbs, Black community, or White community – will typically have an employee group comprising at least 75% Black people (see Table 5.1). Therefore, when you support and patronize Black-owned restaurants and other businesses, you are helping those businesses create and maintain jobs for Black Americans.

Black-owned restaurants have always been an integral part of my life. If I have a breakfast or lunch business meeting, it will likely be at a Black-owned restaurant. Specifically, my Thanksgiving family dinners are catered by Black-owned restaurants. Six years ago, my daughter, Akilah, and I ate at a different Black-owned restaurant each week for a year. It was easy because Chicago has over 100 Black-owned restaurants, making it the city with the most such restaurants in the U.S. And they are not limited to soul food. Some, like Ms. Biscuits, serve breakfast only, or seafood, or vegetarian, or are dine-in, and some, like Cleo's Southern Cusine, are only take-out. My other favorites in Chicago are 5 Loaves Eatery, Chicken & Waffles, Batter & Berries, Luella's Southern Kitchen, and Hecky's Barbecue. And my Black-owned restaurant loyalty extends beyond Chicago. I try to eat at a Black-owned restaurant in every city that I visit. I believe there are few people in the country who have eaten at more Black-owned restaurants than I have. When asked why I do it, my response is "It's a quick, easy way for me to put money into the local Black community."

In addition to eating at restaurants in major cities like New York, Atlanta, and Los Angeles, my restaurant pilgrimages have taken me to Hughley's Southern Cuisine in Honolulu, Gritz Cafe in Las Vegas, Martha Lou's Kitchen in Charleston, and Double D Soul Food in Daytona Beach. I have great stories attached to many of these restaurants. For example, over 15 years ago, a student I taught at Kellogg, Derek Fleming, told me that he was moving to New York City after graduation to start a restaurant with a chef who had recently won as a contestant on a television cooking show. The restaurant was the Red Rooster in Harlem, and the chef was Marcus Samuelsson.

During a business trip to Baltimore three years ago, I went to Terra Cafe, a Black-owned restaurant close to Johns Hopkins University. I Ubered to the location from my downtown hotel. I arrived for breakfast, ignoring their website information that stated they opened for lunch. The door was locked so I knocked and the owner, Terence Dickson, opened it to tell me they were not opening for another three hours. I told him that I was visiting from Chicago. He replied, "Come on in. We will open the kitchen early and cook a delicious breakfast for you!"

Another humorous moment I had was at the Silver Slipper Restaurant in the Roxbury community of Boston. I went there for breakfast, took a seat at the counter, began reading the menu, and said hello to the young man cleaning the tables. I asked him if they served unsweetened iced tea. He smiled and replied, "Oh, you want that diabetic tea!"

One of my most poignant experiences occurred in New Haven, Connecticut. I was there to teach at Yale University during the summer. I Ubered from my downtown hotel to Sandra's Next Generation, where I ate a huge dinner. The food was so delicious that I ordered more to take back to the hotel. My plan was to walk the two miles back to the hotel, which would assist in my digestion of the meal, allowing me to "pig out" on my take-out. I was walking gleefully, almost with a happy skip, savoring the delicious food that I had just devoured, anticipating being even happier after eating my take-out. Then I walked by a homeless man, who said, "You look really happy. I see you went to Sandra's. Are you caring or sharing?" After replying, "Hi back to you," I realized his question stopped me in my tracks. I responded, "I'm sharing with you," and gave him the bag filled with a meal that I knew he would love as much as I had.

This is also the city where my search for a Black-owned restaurant led me to a Black community. The restaurant was filled to capacity with Black patrons. But to my disappointing surprise, there was not even one Black employee, only Black customers. (This is reminiscent of the story mentioned in the Black banking chapter about White banks in Harlem that do not have employees or provide loans to Black depositors.)

My dearest friend, Dawn, was with me. We have traveled the world together, and I sometimes call her Harriet because she is fearless like Harriet Tubman. As we departed, Dawn and I asked to speak to the White owner. After asking him if he employed any Black people, he responded, "No. I can hire who the hell I want!" We told him that it was a shame that he did not believe that was the right thing to do, as well as good business to reciprocate to the Black people in the community by giving at least one Black person a job.

A wonderful aspect of Black-owned restaurants is the familial role they play in their communities. There are many that feed the homeless. For example, the aforementioned Terra Cafe, on the second Sunday of each month, preps, packages, and distributes meals, water, clothing, and care packages to homeless residents of Baltimore. Another example is Turkey Chop, located on the west side of Chicago. Their website states, "Since 2014 we have fed over 275,000 people in need." The owner, Quentin Love, won first prize on the Food Network's reality show *Guy's Grocery Games*. He donated half of the $36,000 prize to United Services

Organization and used the other half to feed men and women who are homeless.[33] The restaurant is closed on Mondays so they are able to serve free meals to the homeless.

White Firms' Commitment

The first national effort by non-Blacks to support Black- and other minority-owned businesses began in 1969. It was the federal government's first time since the failed effort to give 40 acres of land confiscated from the Confederacy to the Black Freedmen in 1865 to do anything that could financially benefit the Black community. On March 6, 1969, President Nixon established the Minority Business Development Agency, a federal government organization created to help Black- and other minority-owned businesses grow and prosper. Part of the agency's task was to ensure that the federal government spent part of its annual budget with these firms.[34]

The year 2020 brought a new movement to support Black-owned businesses. The catalyst for this movement was the killing of George Floyd. Searches on Yelp for Black-owned businesses grew 7,000% between May 25 and July 10.[35] People of all ethnicities contributed to the growth that a lot of Black businesses experienced. More and more lists, apps, and websites have been produced nationally to help spread the word and better shape the narrative about why supporting Black-owned businesses is important.

In addition to the positive responses by individuals, the same has occurred with White-owned businesses. Major firms such as Hyatt Hotels, Chase, Bank of America, PepsiCo, Lowe's, and Netflix have pledged support to Black-owned businesses, some of which includes capital to Black business owners. One of the more groundbreaking initiatives is the 15 Percent Pledge, led by fashion designer Aurora James.[36] The 15 Percent Pledge is a strategy that centers on major retailers committing a minimum of 15% of their shelf space to products from Black-owned businesses. The 15% is not a random number but approximates the percentage of the Black population in America. It is also an amount that should have significant impact, representing the potential for retailers to put $14.5 billion back into Black communities. James calculated the probable impact predicated on 15% of the product budgets of the four major retailers that she called on: Target, Sephora, Shopbop, and Whole Foods. Sephora was the first brand to commit to the pledge and will form an advisory group with James and other Black beauty leaders, in addition to putting more Black-owned brands in stores. As James said, "Black people spend trillions of dollars in this country every year, but yet represent an insignificant fraction of how these companies allocate [their] purchasing power. Many Black people choose to spend money with these businesses, their stores are set up in our communities, and their sponsored posts are targeted to us. If they value our money, then value us as well and show us that we are represented. Take the pledge."[37]

How to Find Black-Owned Businesses: Become a Customer

My contribution to this movement is to provide a better understanding of Black businesses to support, and easy tools for you to use in searching for them. The process outlined below provides clarity, while addressing some of the nuances noted above. The best available tool to research and leverage in your efforts to find Black-owned businesses is the internet. In most consumer-facing transactions, keyword searches are usually what drives the starting point in finding what you are looking for. Business owners work with search engines in social media companies to ensure their internet presence has the right "keywords" that will enable their business to be "discovered" by potential customers like yourself.

Basic Search Approach

If you make the decision to support Black businesses as a regular customer, this is one of the easiest ways to do it. Google partnered with the U.S. Black Chamber of Commerce to enable a business to identify itself as Black-owned as an "attribute" to their business profile for searches.

To execute such a search, first launch a search on Google, then enter the following key words: Black-owned, African American owned baker/florist/restaurant/bookstore. You may need to use more specific language for clarification (e.g., Southern cuisine or soul food for restaurants), or adjust for geography because the search may still yield results that are not Black-owned businesses.

The search method is not foolproof because keywords can be used by any business owner. There may be chain restaurants or non-Black-owned establishments that appear in the search, thus additional criteria may be necessary. This basic search is ideal for small businesses like the ones used in the example above. There are several ways to find what you need online.

National Search Tools

As businesses grow in size, their awareness levels increase. Also, it is common for Black entrepreneurs to join trade associations to network with other business owners. The following search tools are effective for facilitating national searches:

- **Black Enterprise Magazine BE 100s: The Nation's Largest Black Businesses.**[38] *Black Enterprise* magazine is the premier national Black-owned business magazine in the United States. Every year since 1973, they have published a list of the nation's largest Black-owned businesses, categorized by industry.

- **National Minority Supplier Development Council (NMSDC).**[39] The NMSDC is one of the country's leading corporate membership organizations. The NMSDC has a database that allows companies and certified MBEs (Minority Business Enterprise) to connect with one another.
- **U.S. Black Chamber of Commerce Member Directory (USBC).**[40] The USBC supports local African American Chambers of Commerce and business organizations in their work of developing and growing Black enterprises. The member directory allows you to connect with your local Black Chamber of Commerce to find local Black-owned businesses in the specific industries in which you are interested.

Professional Trade Associations

With certain highly skilled professions (e.g., doctor, lawyer, engineer, accountant) there are Black trade associations that serve as resources for their members and other organizations or businesses that seek the services of these professionals. Google has created another search avenue for Black professional organizations. If you enter "Black Professional Organizations" into their search engine, all of the prominent organizations appear. At least 26 professions are listed, including these:

- **The National Medical Association (NMA).**[41] It is the largest and oldest national organization representing African American physicians in the United States.
- **The National Society of Black Engineers (NSBE).**[42] It is one of the largest student-run organizations in the United States, with core activities centered on improving the recruitment and retention of Black and other minority engineers in both academia and industry.

- **The National Association of Black Accountants (NABA).**[43] It is an organization that represents the interests of Black professionals, furthering their educational and professional goals in accounting, finance, and related business areas.
- **The National Dental Association (NDA).**[44] It is a professional Association of minority dentists based in Washington, D.C., operating in the United States, Canada, and Latin America.
- **The National Bar Association.**[45] Founded in 1925, it is the nation's largest and oldest national network of predominantly African American attorneys and judges.
- **The National Association of Real Estate Brokers (NAREB).**[46] It is a professional real estate organization that includes members from multiple disciplines in the real estate industry. The national goal is to bring together the nation's minority professionals in the real estate industry to promote the meaningful exchange of ideas about our business and how best to serve our clientele.

As described above, to execute the search, first launch a Google search, then enter "Black Professional Organizations," and when those appear, select the organization you are inquiring about. Alternatively, you could enter "Black" or "African American" and then the name of the profession you are seeking. Again, Google has provided the most efficient way to conduct this search.

Regional Search Tools

If your search needs are not met from a national perspective, there are regional newspapers and business publications that provide an annual list of Black-owned businesses. Crain's does an excellent job of publishing their annual top minority-owned businesses list.[47] The report includes the name, address, website, type of business, ownership status, number of employees, and other relevant data concerning Black-owned businesses. Crain's publishes their list in several large metropolitan areas, including Chicago, Cleveland, Detroit, and New York. Crain's is a paid site, meaning you need a subscription to access the report. To execute that search, first launch a Google search, then enter "Crain's Annual Top Minority-Owned Businesses" followed by the city (Chicago, Cleveland, Detroit, or New York).

Local Search Tools

An additional resource to use for locating small Black businesses is Black newspapers. Black newspapers and Black journalism in general have been integral to the advancement of Black interests in America. The National Newspaper Publishers Association (NNPA) is a trade association of more than 200 African American–owned community newspapers from around the United States since its founded in 1940.[48] On their website you can find 30 states represented with links to their local Black newspapers. To give you an example, the *Dallas Weekly* publishes their own annual list entitled "The Best of Black Dallas."[49] They categorize Black-owned businesses by food and dining, health and fitness, automotive, medical, and other interests.

To execute that search, first launch a Google search, then enter "National Newspaper Publishers Association" or nnpa.org, then click on "About NNPA," then "Current Members," then select the newspaper in the state you are interested in, and then navigate to the business or shop small business section.

As I reach the end of this chapter, I hope that I have raised your awareness of the necessity for supporting Black-owned businesses and provided simple tools that can be used to answer the question from many of my White friends, "How can I find Black-owned companies?" Khadijah Robinson, founder of the Nile List, an online directory of Black-owned businesses, said, "I want to make buying Black normalized in part of people's daily routines."[50] That too, is my aspiration. If Black-owned businesses are to continue to grow, create more jobs, and provide the other benefits mentioned earlier in this chapter to the Black community, they need more White customers. Ideally, those White customers will make spending money with Black-owned businesses a regular practice and not a one-time-only transaction.

Notes

1. Ramos, Manny. "'Shop Black' Campaign Brings Customers to Chatham Businesses." *Chicago Sun Times*. November 27, 2020. https://chicago.suntimes.com/business/2020/11/27/21723386/shop-black-owned-business-friday-customers-holiday-shopping-chatham

2. Haas, Dylan. "How to Find and Support Black-Owned Businesses – and Why it's Important." Mashable. June 18, 2020. https://mashable.com/article/how-to-find-and-support-black-owned-businesses/

3. Sewing, Joy. "Christopher John Rogers and Sergio Hudson for Inauguration." *Houston Chronicle*. January 20, 2021. https://www.houstonchronicle.com/life/article/Kamala-Harris-wears-Black-designer-for-15884829.php

4. Cobler, Paul. "VP Kamala Harris' Inauguration Day Outfit Was Designed by Baton Rouge Native Christopher John Rogers." *Advocate*. January 20, 2021. https://www.theadvocate.com/baton_rouge/entertainment_life/article_66a54e18-5b3b-11eb-95b1-0f13b17cdaec.html

5. Lockwood, Lisa. "VP Kamala Harris' Choice of Christopher John Rogers Garners Most Media Impact Value." WWD. January 21, 2021. https://wwd.com/fashion-news/designer-luxury/vp-kamala-harris-choice-of-christopher-john-rogers-garners-most-media-impact-value-1234706758/

6. Robinson, Nandi, and R.L. LaMore. "Why Buy Local? An Assessment of the Economic Advantages of Shopping at Locally Owned Businesses." Michigan State University Center for Community and Economic Development. September 2010. https://community-wealth.org/content/why-buy-local-assessment-economic-advantage-shopping-locally-owned-businesses

7. Ramos, Manny. "'Shop Black' Campaign Brings Customers to Chatham Businesses." *Chicago Sun Times*. November 27, 2020. https://chicago.suntimes.com/business/2020/11/27/21723386/shop-black-owned-business-friday-customers-holiday-shopping-chatham

8. "Dave Chappelle Set to Turn Ohio Firehouse into Comedy Club." Associated Press. December 30, 2020. https://apnews.com/article/ohio-fires-dave-chappelle-dayton-a6bd76109487e0f013c0d80563b89578

9. Alexander, Keith L. "Who Is Robert Smith? A Quiet Billionaire Makes Some Noise with $20 Million Gift to the African American Museum." *Washington Post*. September 24, 2016. https://www.washingtonpost.com/national/who-is-this-robert-smith-a-quiet-billionaire-makes-some-noise-with-20-million-gift-to-the-african-american-museum/2016/09/23/547da3a8-6fd0-11e6-8365-b19e428a975e_story.html

10. Jackson, Cheryl V. "When Building Your Business Means Hiding That It's Black-Owned." *Chicago Tribune*. April 14, 2016. https://www.chicagotribune.com/business/blue-sky/ct-black-entrepreneurs-downplay-ownership-bsi-20160414-story.html

11. Griswold, Alison. "You Could Buy Anything from the Sears Catalog – Even a House." Quartz. October 20, 2018. https://qz.com/1429145/you-could-buy-anything-from-the-sears-catalog-even-a-house/

12. Farzan, Antonia N. "Sears's 'Radical' Past: How Mail-Order Catalogues Subverted the Racial Hierarchy of Jim Crow." *Washington Post*. https://www.washingtonpost.com/news/morning-mix/wp/2018/10/16/searss-radical-past-how-mail-order-catalogues-subverted-the-racial-hierarchy-of-jim-crow/

13. "Bio for Valerie Daniels-Carter." Valerie Daniels-Carter personal page. Accessed January 2, 2021. https://www.valeriedanielscarter.com/home

14. Fannin, Mike. "The Truth in Black and White: An Apology from the Kansas City Star." *Kansas City Star*. December 20, 2020. https://www.kansascity.com/news/local/article247928045.html

15. Tolly, Victor. "Chicago Defender (1905 -)." Black Past. January 11, 2008. https://www.blackpast.org/african-american-history/chicago-defender-1905/

16. Michaeli, Ethan. "Bound for the Promised Land." *Atlantic*. https://www.theatlantic.com/politics/archive/2016/01/chicago-defender/422583/

17. Ibid.

18. Parry, Tyler. "The Curious History of Anthony Johnson: From Captive African to Right-Wing Talking Point." Black Perspectives. July 22, 2019. https://www.aaihs.org/the-curious-history-of-anthony-johnson-from-captive-african-to-right-wing-talking-point/

19. Springgs, William E. "Here's Some History to Help Understand the Racial Wealth Gap." AFL-CIO. January 22, 2016. https://aflcio.org/2016/1/22/heres-some-history-help-understand-racial-wealth-gap

20. "Francis 'Free Frank' McWorter." Springfield's Sculptures, Monuments, and Plaques. Accessed January 2, 2021. http://springfieldsculptures.net/McWorter.html

21. "John Berry Meachum (1789-1854)." Black Past. July 29, 2014. https://www.blackpast.org/african-american-history/meachum-john-berry-1789-1854/

22. "Robert 'Black Bob' Renfro: Tennessee's First Black Entrepreneur." Nashville History. February 20, 2020. https://nashvillehistory.blogspot.com/2020/02/robert-black-bob-renfro-tennessees.html

23. Lartey, James, and Sam Morris. "How White Americans Used Lynchings to Terrorize and Control Black People." *Guardian*. April 26, 2018. https://www.theguardian.com/us-news/2018/apr/26/lynchings-memorial-us-south-montgomery-alabama

24. "The People's Grocery Lynchings (Thomas Moss, Will Stewart, Calvin McDowell)." Lynching Sites Project Memphis. Accessed January 2, 2021. https://lynchingsitesmem.org/lynching/peoples-grocery-lynchings-thomas-moss-will-stewart-calvin-mcdowell

25. Barclay, Dolores, Todd Lewan, and Allen G. Breed. "Prosperity Made Blacks a Target for Land Grabs." *Los Angeles Times*. December 9, 2001. https://www.latimes.com/archives/la-xpm-2001-dec-09-mn-13043-story.html

26. Gara, Antoine. "The Bezos of Black Wall Street." *Forbes*. June 18, 2020. https://www.forbes.com/sites/antoinegara/2020/06/18/the-bezos-of-black-wall-street-tulsa-race-riots-1921/?sh=617bcb52f321

27. "On This Date in History, May 31, 1921: The Tulsa Race Riot." America's Black Holocaust Museum. June 1, 2013. https://www.abhmuseum.org/on-this-date-in-history-may-31-1921-the-tulsa-race-riot/

28. Elliott, Dominique. "Remembering the Excellence in Black Wall Street." Fayetteville State University Press. February 24, 2017. https://www.fsuthevoice.com/remembering-the-excellence-in-black-wall-street/

29. Staples, Brent. "The Haunting of Tulsa, Okla." *New York Times*. December 26, 2020. https://www.nytimes.com/2020/12/26/opinion/tulsa-race-massacre-mass-grave.html

30. Cecelski, David S., and Timothy B. Tyson, eds. *Democracy Betrayed: The Wilmington Race Riot of 1898 and Its Legacy*. UNC Press Books, 2000, pp. 15–41.

31. Crain, Caleb. "What a White-Supremacist Coup Looks Like." *New Yorker*. April 20, 2020. https://www.newyorker.com/magazine/2020/04/27/what-a-white-supremacist-coup-looks-like

32. Wormser, Richard. *The Rise and Fall of Jim Crow: The Companion to the PBS Television Series*. Macmillan, 2004, pp. 85–86.

33. "Chef Quentin Love Donates Half of Food Network Winnings to Feed Chicago's Hungry." Good Black News. December 27, 2015. https://good-blacknews.org/2015/12/27/chef-quentin-love-donates-half-of-food-network-winnings-to-feed-chicagos-hungry/

34. "The History of the MBDA." Minority Business Development Agency. Accessed January 27, 2021. https://www.mbda.gov/about/history

35. Gross, Elana L. "Support for Black-Owned Businesses Increases More Than 7,000%, Yelp Reports." *Forbes*. July 22, 2020. https://www.forbes.com/sites/elanagross/2020/07/22/support-for-black-owned-businesses-increases-more-than-7000-yelp-reports/?sh=10dcfd2b42a8

36. Hess, Liam. "Aurora James on Her 15 Percent Pledge Campaign to Support Black-Owned Businesses." *Vogue*. June 6, 2020. https://www.vogue.com/article/aurora-james-brother-vellies-15-percent-pledge-small-business-spotlight

37. Hyde, Shelby. "Aurora James' 15 Percent Pledge Is Calling All Major Retailers to Help Level the Playing Field for Black Businesses." Zoe Report. June 5, 2020. https://www.thezoereport.com/p/aurora-james-15-percent-pledge-is-calling-all-major-retailers-to-help-level-the-playing-field-for-black-businesses-22959243

38. "BE 100s: The Nation's Largest Black Businesses." *Black Enterprise*. Accessed January 2, 2021. https://www.blackenterprise.com/be100s/top100/

39. "National Minority Supplier Development Council." NMSDC Homepage. Accessed January 2, 2021. https://nmsdc.org/

40. "USBC Chambers Directory." US Black Chambers, Inc. Accessed January 2, 2021. https://usblackchambers.org/usbc-chambers/

41. National Medical Association. Accessed January 2, 2021. https://www.nmanet.org/

42. National Society of Black Engineers. Accessed January 2, 2021. https://www.nsbe.org/home.aspx

43. National Association of Black Accountants. Accessed January 2, 2021. https://www.nabainc.org/

44. National Dental Association. Accessed January 2, 2021. https://ndaonline.org/

45. National Bar Association. Accessed January 2, 2021. https://nationalbar.org/

46. National Association of Real Estate Brokers. Accessed January 2, 2021. https://www.nareb.com/

47. "Crain's List 2020." Chicago Business. Accessed January 2, 2021. https://www.chicagobusiness.com/crains-list/chicagos-biggest-minority-owned-businesses-2020

48. National Newspaper Publishers Association. Accessed January 2, 2021. https://nnpa.org/

49. "The Best of Black Dallas 2020." *Dallas Weekly*. Accessed January 2, 2021. https://www.dallasweekly.com/dallas-weeklys-best-of-black-dallas-2020/#//

50. Albrecht, Leslie. "5 Ways to Support Black-Owned Businesses: It's Not Rocket Science – People Just Choose Not to Do It." Market Watch. June 19, 2020. https://www.marketwatch.com/story/a-starter-guide-to-supporting-black-owned-businesses-its-not-rocket-science-people-just-choose-not-to-do-it-2020-06-15

CHAPTER SIX

Write a Letter Supporting Reparations

White people should think of reparations as a poker game where somebody has been cheating. . . . If somebody said I've been cheating the whole game and now I'm going to stop cheating, wouldn't you want your money back?[1]

I AM ASKING you to write a letter to your federal congressional representative demanding cash payments for reparations to Black Americans who are the descendants of Blacks enslaved from 1619 to 1865. This is a debt owed and past due.

> We've come to our nation's capital to cash a check. When the architects of our Republic wrote the magnificent words of the Constitution and the Declaration of Independence, they were signing a promissory note to which every American was to fall heir. . . . Instead of honoring this sacred obligation, America has given the Negro people a bad check, a check which has

come back marked "insufficient funds." But we refuse to believe that bank of justice is bankrupt.[2]

These were the words of Dr. Martin Luther King Jr. from his famous "I Have a Dream" speech given at the March on Washington in 1963. Dr. King's effulgent use of the extended metaphor of a financial promissory note due to Black Americans was perfect. Like Dr. King, I believe the "bank of justice," America's government, should pay the balance due on this promissory note. The payment should be in cash and equal to the amount needed to close the wealth gap between Blacks and Whites that is the direct consequence of slavery, Black codes, and redlining mentioned in previous chapters of this book.

However, we must confront the fact that the idea of paying reparations to Blacks for these previous crimes against them has never been supported by most Whites. In a 2019 survey by the Associated Press, only 15% of Whites supported reparations, compared to 74% of Blacks.[3] But justice should never be determined by a popular vote. Rather, the obligation to do the right thing should be the ruling determinant. Revealingly, most Americans did not support the abolition of slavery. Nevertheless, President Lincoln decided to do the right thing when he signed the Emancipation Proclamation to end slavery. (Admittedly, he also did it for strategic reasons, primarily to weaken the Confederacy.)

Another great example of a government deciding to do the right thing, despite the lack of popular support, was the decision of the German government to pay reparations to Jewish victims of Nazi crimes. They have paid over $89 billion in reparations over 60 years.[4] Many Germans showed their opposition to these payments through violence. They were vehemently against paying anything to Jews. In fact, over 70% of Germans opposed reparation payments. Despite this mountain of opposition, the German government signed a reparations agreement with the government of Israel in 1952. Roman Kent, a survivor of Auschwitz who was involved in the negotiations, made the following statement: "We survivors and the Germans of today are together united. . . . Both of us do not want our past to be our children's future."[5]

Unfortunately, the absence of reparations payments to Blacks has made our troubled past with Whites, especially the government, a major factor contributing to the horrible present condition that Blacks live in today. The wealth gap that is an intentional and maliciously created reality of our present has a continued and negative affect on the future of the children who are descendants and victims of slavery, the Black codes, and redlining. Those descendants today are still burdened by the unfairness that their ancestors endured. An illuminating point is that even when we are more educated than Whites, Blacks have less financial stability. We are forever trying to dig ourselves out of the financial holes that result from virtually no transference of generational wealth. This is demonstrated in the research of economists Sandy Darity and Darrick Hamilton, who concluded that inheritance and other forms of intergenerational transfer account for more of the wealth gap than any other demographic in socioeconomic indicators.[6] In 2014, Brandeis University did a study indicating that almost 50% of White households received financial transfers from other relatives, compared to 10% for Black households.[7] One result of this disparity is that Whites with only high school degrees have greater wealth than Blacks with college degrees, and Whites with bachelor's degrees have greater wealth than Blacks with master's degrees. One study that reveals the power of inheritance over education is found in the research at Duke University that highlights that a family headed by a Black college graduate has less wealth, on average, than a family headed by a White high school dropout.[8] It is my belief that for the good of the country, this wealth gap can and must be eliminated through well-placed and well-deserved reparations.

Reparations History

The belief that financial reparations are due to Blacks is not new. Dating back to slavery, Blacks have always known that it was wrong for them to be enslaved and made to work without compensation. Sadly, that particular wrong, the denial of financial recompense, has never been righted. Inexplicably, there has always seemed to be a coldheartedness on the part of most Whites to financially assist Blacks.

When people were freed from slavery, the government did not give them a penny. The only effort to compensate or give reparations to formerly enslaved people began two years after the signing of the Emancipation Proclamation. In the winter of 1865, as the Union Army was defeating the Confederates, many formerly enslaved people began marching with and following Union soldiers. They were taking refuge. Union Army leaders did not know what to do with this group, estimated to upwards of 17,000 people. They told President Lincoln about their dilemma. In return he sent the following question via messenger from Washington, D.C., to General William Tecumseh Sherman in Savannah, Georgia, "What do these Negros want?"[9] To get an answer, General Sherman met with 20 Black religious leaders on January 12, 1865.[10] Their congregations ranged from 200 to 1,800 members. All of the leaders were men. They ranged in age from 26 to 72; 5 were free born and 15 had been enslaved, while 9 of the 15 were newly freed men, having been enslaved until, in their words, "the Union forces freed me" and "the time the Union Army came in." Their average number of years enslaved were 45.6 years, with the shortest time at 25 years, and the longest at 72 years. Three had purchased their freedom. After 28 years of enslavement, Abraham Burke paid $800 for his freedom and Garrison Frazier, the elected spokesman for the group, paid $1,000 in gold and silver to purchase the freedom for him and his wife, after 59 years of enslavement.

Their Christian denominations were Methodist, Episcopal, or Baptist. The latter included the First Baptist Church, the Missionary Baptist Church, the Second African Baptist Church, and the Third African Baptist Church. These men wanted financial security for Blacks. Frazier told Sherman that he defined slavery as one person "receiving by irresistible power the work of another man, and not by his consent" and went on to tell Sherman that freedom meant "placing us where we could reap the fruit of our own labor, and take care of ourselves." The best way to accomplish this was "to have land, and turn it and till it by our own labor."[11] Sherman asked the group if they would rather integrate into the general society or live separately. The youngest member of the group, 26-year-old James Lynch, who was free born, voiced his support for the former. The other 19 men voted for the latter with their full support of Frazier, who responded, "I would prefer to live by ourselves, for there is a prejudice against us in the South that will take years to get over." As the Black codes and redlining would show, his pragmatic statement was in many ways prophetic.

The lone attempt of the U.S. government to provide reparations to Blacks was approved four days after this historic meeting, known as Field Order No. 15.[12] The order had the objective of giving land to the four million newly freed people so that they could begin the process of living an independent life as farmers or anything else they desired. The land identified for parceling out was 400,000 acres along the coasts of South Carolina, Georgia, and Florida. These acres had previously been owned by

Confederate landowners who lost the Civil War and were to be tried for treason. This land confiscated by the U.S. government was to be sold, via legal title, to former enslaved Blacks. According to Mehrsa Baradaran's *The Color of Money*, The Freedmen's Bureau Act of 1865 formalized Sherman's field order into a law "providing that each negro might have forty acres at a low price on long credit." The order came directly from President Lincoln, who wished to give freed slaves "an interest in the soil." The price of land was to be fixed at $1.25 per acre, 40% of which was due up front.[13]

This was a major act of the government to help put Blacks on the path to creating wealth for themselves, but unfortunately this well-intentioned and well-deserved act of reparations was short lived. Less than three months after Field Order No. 15 was enacted, Lincoln was assassinated by John Wilkes Booth, who shouted, "Sic semper tyrannis! [Ever thus to tyrants!] The South is avenged."[14] His diary demonstrated his disdain for Lincoln abolishing slavery and a belief that Lincoln "was made the tool of the North to crush out, or try to crush out slavery."[15] His hatred of Lincoln seemed to emanate from a hatred of Blacks, whom he referred to as "monkeys," "apes," or "thick-skulled darkies," and he believed that Blacks were made solely to help enrich Whites – "this country was formed for the white not for the black man," and that slavery was "one of the greatest blessings that God ever bestowed upon a favored nation."[16] The murder of Lincoln effectively killed Field Order No. 15 and its role in reparations for Blacks.

In a cruel twist of fate, a White pro-slavery Southerner who had more interest in helping former Confederate landowners and soldiers than Black people succeeded Lincoln. The new president was Andrew Johnson, who was a slaveowner and had been Lincoln's vice president. Under his presidency, instead of penalizing the former Confederates for treason, some by hanging, he granted them freedom via presidential pardons. His last pardon was to Jefferson Davis, the former Confederate president. More pointedly, President Johnson returned the lands confiscated by the Union army. This was the land that had begun to be distributed to the four million newly freed Black people. Over 40,000 Black people had received land, but it was all taken back by the government.[17]

Johnson's Amnesty Proclamation was signed on May 29, 1865, and stated that the "restoration of all rights of property, except as to slaves" was to be returned to former Confederate soldiers.[18] Johnson expressed clear disdain for the idea of awarding reparations of any kind to Blacks when he scoffed at the recommendation that the White Southern landowners should be legally required to provide a small homestead for each of the people they formerly enslaved. The idea was the proposition of General Oliver Howard who said that Johnson "was amused and gave no heed to this recommendation."[19]

Johnson's response was not a surprise. Even after the Emancipation Proclamation was signed in 1863, Johnson, as vice president, gave a speech that clearly stated his feelings about Blacks. He said, "I was then, as I am now, for a White man's government, and for a free, intelligent, White constituency, instead of a Negro aristocracy."[20] Despite the efforts of Generals Sherman and Howard to transfer land to Blacks, it all quickly came to a halt in the fall of 1865 with the order of President Johnson. He successfully diverted any commitment of the federal government away from giving anything to Black people.

The U.S. Precedent of Paying Out Reparations

W.E.B Du Bois would later describe Johnson's reversal of the efforts of Lincoln and Sherman and the Reconstruction Era in the following fashion: "the slave went free; stood a brief moment in the sun; then moved back again toward slavery."[21] While the government refused to give Blacks anything, that same government paid reparations to former slave owners. A total payout of $896,700 was given to 979 former slave owners for 2,989 former enslaved people who were valued at $300 each.[22] In a startling similarity to an event a few decades earlier, in 1834, the British government showed the same empathy to White slave owners. They abolished slavery in their Caribbean colonies, with payments totaling £20 million ($26 million) to over 40,000 White slave owners.[23] This practice of only paying reparations to non-Blacks continued. While I detest the fact that White former slave owners received reparations, I am happy to report that non-Black people of color have received financial reparations for government-inflicted wounds. Those people included Native Americans, native Hawaiians, and Japanese Americans.

In 1920, the U.S government, via the Hawaiian Homes Commission Act, gave land leases to people who were at least 50% native Hawaiian. The cost was $1 for a 99-year lease.[24] This reparation was given as restitution for the federal government's action dating back to 1893, when it took massive acres of land from native Hawaiians.

On the mainland, Native Americans also received reparations for the endless number of crimes the federal government inflicted on their people. One of the most egregious acts was the taking of their land. Through the Indian Claims Commission enacted in 1946, only $1.3 billion was awarded to Native Americans. The payout averaged $1,000 per person and was given to 176 tribes.[25]

Four decades later, the government paid compensation to Japanese Americans for imprisoning them during World War II.[26] One descendant of those American citizens detained for several years because of their race is Robyn Syphax. Syphax is a strong advocate for reparations, arguing that that they be paid to her Black family members and herself. She has witnessed the positive impact of financial reparations when they are paid to people who have suffered intentional harm from the government. Her maternal grandparents, Jayne and Mitsuo Yamamoto, are Japanese Americans who received $20,000 each in reparations from the U.S government in 1988.[27]

As a backdrop to Ms. Syphax's family story, in 1942, the U.S was at war with Germany, Italy, and Japan. Specifically, the government labeled all Americans of Japanese descendant as potential enemies. The same designation was not applied to Americans of German or Italian descent. Over 120,000 Japanese Americans were forced by the government to leave their homes and live in internment camps, surrounded by barbed wire fences and with armed guards focused on the people inside of those fences. The Yamamotos were among those interned.

Forty-six years later, the Civil Liberties Act was approved by the U.S. Congress in 1988. It apologized to Japanese Americans and agreed to pay $20,000 each to compensate more than 80,000 Japanese Americans who were formally imprisoned.[28] Mitsuo Yamamoto qualified for the reparation payment because he was 16 years old when he was imprisoned. He said, "You should pay for your mistakes," and that "the payment of cash made the apology feel more sincere."[29] The only payment received by Japanese Americans prior to the reparations check was given when they were freed from prison. It was $25 cash and a one-way train ticket to their destination.[30]

A year after the Civil Liberties Act was passed, a bill was introduced in Congress asking that the government convene a study on reparations to Black Americans; it did not pass. The same bill has been submitted to Congress for 32 consecutive years and has never passed.[31] While the first formal request for reparations from the federal government occurred in 1989, Blacks have always sought financial redress for enslavement dating back to 1783. A formerly enslaved woman, Belinda Sutton, petitioned the court of Massachusetts to recompense her with a life's pension. Her successful request for reparations was to be paid from the estate of Isaac Royall. The Royall family had held Belinda in bondage. She was emancipated after Isaac Royall fled Massachusetts and returned to England during the Revolutionary War. Belinda, who had been enslaved for 50 years, claimed that part of the assets owned by Isaac Royall should be paid to her because his estate "was partly a product of her own uncompensated labor."[32] Belinda prevailed, and the court ordered an annual payment of £15 and 12 shillings. While this story has a wonderful ending, the story of Belinda Sutton is an aberration.

A little over a century later, in 1896, a similar request for a pension from the government was requested by 600,000 people who were formally enslaved.[33] They were members of the National Ex-Slave Mutual Relief, Bounty, and Pension Association. The leaders of this movement were Isaiah Dickerson and Callie House, who had both been enslaved. Unfortunately, their efforts to get reparations were not successful.

Virtually every Black person who has requested reparations of some kind has been denied. An example is the case of Matilda McCrear. As a two-year-old, she was taken from Africa with her mother and 108 other Africans. She was held hostage on a boat called the *Clotilda* for 45 days as it crossed the Atlantic Ocean and landed in Alabama. This was a crime against humanity as well as a crime against federal laws, since federal government outlawed the slave trade voyages in 1808.[34]

Matilda's given name was "Àbáké," meaning "born to be loved by all" in the Yoruba language.[35] But a loving life for Àbáké was taken away by the barbarism of slavery. In Africa, her father was killed; during the middle passage, her cousin died; and once they arrived in America, her sisters were sold to a different slave owner. She was enslaved in America and had her first child at the age of 14 by a White man.

Matilda never forgot this cruel, unfair, hard start to her life and that she suffered for the sole purpose of enriching Whites. She never believed that apologies or "letting bygones be bygones" was enough. At the least, she wanted financial reparations. When her grandsons informed her in 1931 that retired military veterans from World War I had received financial bonuses for their past service, she took action. She believed that she was entitled to something similar, so, at the age of 73, this brave, tough, and proud woman began her journey seeking government reparations. She walked 70 miles from her home to the Dallas County courthouse in Selma, Alabama, to request payment for her family's enslavement. An article in the Selma newspaper said:

> An old African woman in the Court House corridor, patiently waiting her turn to see the Probate Judge. Her name was Tildy McCrear. She bore the mark of an African tribe on her left cheek. Tildy pointed to the symbol with pride. It was the crowning proof of her contention that she was a pure-blooded African who had come to America aboard the last slave ship to smuggle in a cargo of Negroes.
>
> Tildy believed that being snatched from her home in Africa, while yet an infant, called for a little reimbursement. After the judge dismissed her claim and sent her away to live the rest of her life in poverty, she thanked him "with grand courtesy," adding: "I don't spec I needs anything more 'n I got."[36]

Like most Blacks in America, Matilda got no redress from the government and inherited nothing from her mother, Grace. Matilda, in turn, left no inheritances to her children or grandchildren. In contrast, descendants of Timothy Meaher, the financier of the *Clotilda*, a boat that cost him $35,000, have prospered. He illegally stole Matilda and 109 other Black people, gained wealth from selling them, and transferred that wealth to future generations. The Meaher Family now has assets of at least $25 million. They have never shared any of that wealth with Matilda's descendants or any of the other descendants of people who enriched them. This absence of wealth sharing has not been ignored by the Black descendants. They rightfully believe they are owed financial compensation. One descendant stated, "I think it would be equitable for them to make some payment to the descendants of the Clotilda cargo."[37]

Unlike the Meaher family, there are a few White families who have shared their inherited wealth with the descendants of people enslaved by their forebears. One such person is Phoebe Kilby. After discovering that her family created wealth by enslaving Black people, she took action. She met some of the descendants of those enslaved people and endowed scholarships for their grandchildren. One of those Black descendants is Betty Kilby, a professional writer and a plaintiff in Virginia's school desegregation case in the 1950s. She and Phoebe are also blood relatives and close friends. When asked why she did what she did, Phoebe responded, "We could wait for Congress or we can listen to the express desires of our African American cousins and respond directly ourselves."[38]

Another White person who responded directly to the call for reparations was Felicia Furman. She is a descendent of Richard and James Furman. The oldest private university in South Carolina, Furman University, is named after Richard Furman, while the school's first president was his son, James.[39] Both men enslaved Black people and were ardent opponents of abolition. The same sentiment applied to most of the people associated with the school in the 1800s. In fact, the school was closed from 1861 to 1865 because most of its students and faculty enlisted in the Confederate Army.

In addition to being related to these men, Felicia Furman is directly related to the enslavement of Black people. Her family history spans over 200 years of reaping the financial rewards of unpaid labor at the Woodlands, the family plantation, dating back to the 1700s. As reparations to the descendants of those held in bondage at the Woodlands, Furman took a portion of the inheritance that she received and created a family scholarship fund. She acknowledged that she deserves no special recognition for giving back some of the money made through the free labor of others. The reparations she made that are most gratifying to me are the truths that she has shared about the actions of her family. For example, she said that her family passed down through multiple generations the lie that they gave 40 acres to formerly enslaved people at the Woodlands. She said the truth, which came from research, is that the land was never given for free, but that the former enslaved people paid for it.[40]

While I am not a big proponent of scholarships as reparations, I am happy for the descendants if that is what they want. I support more strongly the same form of reparations that was given to Jews and Japanese Americans: CASH! History tells us that cash works, producing positive outcomes. As stated earlier in this chapter, Mitsuo Yamamoto firmly believed that the addition of cash made the government's apology legitimate. It also, undeniably, closes some of the wealth gap.

Reparations in the form of cash have an impact on the recipient and future generations. Scholarships, on the other hand, cannot be leveraged to purchase greater valued assets such as homes. Cash provides a down payment that can be used to procure a mortgage for a home nine times greater than the down payment.

This home can then become an asset that can be transferred to succeeding generations. That is how wealth is built.

A great example of the positive impact that cash reparations can command goes back to the Civil War and Robert Smalls, a formally enslaved man who received $1,500 in 1862 for steering a boat from the Confederates to the Union, whereupon he gained his freedom.[41] He used the money to open a store, build a local school for children, and purchase the home previously owned by the people who had enslaved him and his family. Multiple generations of his family lived in the home for almost 100 years, from 1863 to 1953.

One person who lived in the home was its former owner, Mrs. McKee. She and her husband owned the home, but lost it due to unpaid taxes. Robert Smalls purchased the empty home. McKee, who was an elderly woman suffering with dementia, returned. Smalls let her live in the home with his family until she died.

The positive impact of Robert Smalls receiving $1,500 resonates today. His great-great-grandson Michael Boulware Moore said, "It's a gift for us to be connected to Robert and his legacy." His great-great granddaughter Helen Boulware Moore said, "Absolutely an inspiration! If you look at the descendants you can see it because of what we have done educationally. Many of us are involved with education ourselves – gotten doctorate degrees, been physicians and ministers."[42]

The home received National Historic Landmark designation in 1974, in recognition of Smalls's great service to the country.[43] He joined the Union Army and fought in 17 battles against the Confederates. He was also responsible for the enlistment of 5,000 Blacks into the Union Army. After the war, he served the country as an elected member of the Senate and Congress, where he served for five terms. Finally, he wrote the bill that created free public education for Americans. He died in his home in 1915, and the house was inherited by his descendants.

Robert Smalls's story is a perfect example of the things that happened over a century ago having an impact on people today. The money that he received from the government is directly related to the success of his descendants today. The same applies to White Americans. Their financial success today can be directly attributed to what happened 70 years ago with redlining, what happened 150 years ago with the Black Codes, and with what happened 400 years ago with the beginning of slavery. Therefore, I am imploring Whites to embrace the supportive positions of other Whites, including Felicia Furman, who said, "Making reparations is central to creating a society based on equality. Without reparations and an official apology, we will make no headway;"[44] Graziella Bertocchi, an Italian economist, who said, "Slavery remains a persistent determinant of today's inequality;"[45] and, finally, Seth Cohen, a journalist, who said, "By ultimately paying, the United States can write a historic wrong while building a stronger and more equitable future."[46]

While I am asking individuals to support reparations, I am happy to report that following the death of George Floyd, more mainstream news media have been more direct and public in their support. Here are a few headline examples:

1. **Reparations Now: Why White People Must Join the Call to Pay Reparations for Slavery** (*Forbes*)[47]
2. **Durham Calls for Federal Reparations for the Descendants of Enslaved People** (*News & Observer*)[48]
3. **Reparations to Black Americans for Slavery Gain New Attention** (*Wall Street Journal*)[49]
4. **"Uncomfortable Truth": The Push for a Slavery Reparations Commission in Congress** (*Washington Post*)[50]

HEAD: Making Reparations Work

With an increased interest in supporting reparations has come the increased interest in to how it would work. Here is my proposal, which is pragmatic, affordable, simple, and will result in closing the wealth gap between most Black and White Americans. It is not paternalistic, needlessly complicated, or too expensive. It would cost approximately $3 trillion, which is 15% of the country's annual economy of $20 trillion. That $3 trillion is less than the 2008 bank bailouts, which amounted to more than $4 trillion.[51]

In response to a question regarding the cost of reparations, Professor Edward Baptist, who is White and a historian at Cornell University, said, "Whites have little claim to say that something is too much to pay. They have no standing to argue that the wealth distribution should remain where it is today. There's no justifiable way – in my opinion – to make that argument."[52]

The wealth gap between Blacks and Whites would almost immediately close with my proposal that reparations be paid in one check to the approximate 20 million Black Americans, 18 years and over, who are descendants of Black people who were enslaved in the United States. The amount of each check would be the same, $153,000, which is the average difference between Black and White net worth. In addition to closing the wealth gap, this reparation payment would heal many of the country's racial problems that stem from the chronic state of poverty intentionally placed on Blacks by the government. This check would directly address the problem cited by Rue Simmons, the alderwoman in Evanston who led the successful effort passed on March 22, 2021, for the city to agree to pay reparations to some of its Black residents. She said, "There is a 400-year head start in the white community . . . wealth [that] was established in the slave trade that has passed down from generation to generation. There's no amount of hard work, bootstrapping, work ethic, education that can uplift the black community collectively to a place of equality."[53] She concluded, and I completely agree, that the only means to that equality are reparations.

Therefore, I am making an earnest request of you to join us in support of reparations, be it my proposal or another. Your willingness to actively support reparations would put you in the "Walter Vaughan" club. He was a White newspaper editor in the early 1890s who sought reparations for Blacks formerly enslaved. He published a document and sold copies for a dollar each, imploring the government to pay a pension to people held in bondage before the Emancipation Proclamation. The pamphlet was titled, "Freedmen's Pension Bill: A Plea for American Freedom."[54]

Like Walter, your reparations support can begin by supporting H.R. 40, the bill proposed by former Michigan Congressman John Conyers.[55] The number 40 in the bill represents 40 acres that the four million formerly enslaved people never received. This bill, written by Rep. Conyers, proposes a federally funded study and development of proposals for reparations, at a proposed cost of $12 million for the study and proposals. He wrote it in 1989, a year after the government agreed to pay reparations to Japanese Americans. He proposed the bill for 28 consecutive years, including 2017, the year he retired. On January 19, 2019, Congresswoman Sheila Jackson Lee of Texas proposed the same 14-page bill. It had 169 sponsors, all of whom were Democrats, but it did not pass. The same bill was again proposed on June 19, 2020, following George Floyd's murder; it did not pass.

Rep. Jackson Lee again proposed the bill on January 4, 2021. A call to support this bill comes from as far away as Germany's Susan Neiman, the director of the Einstein Forum. She describes herself as a Jewish White woman born in America, but she has lived most of her adult life in Berlin. It is her assertion that the model used by the governments of East and West Germany to pay reparations to Jews for the Holocaust must be duplicated by the U.S. government to repay Blacks for slavery. She emphatically stated, "We must urge Congress to pass H.R. 40 so that our engagement with the past will deepen, and bear fruit."[56] Here is a template of a letter that you can use to write to your congressional representative expressing your support of H.R. 40:

> Dear Senator XXX and Representative XXX:
>
> As you consider legislative action on closing the Black/ White wealth gap, I am writing to urge your support for reparations to Black Americans. Providing reparations to Black Americans, who are descendants of people enslaved in America, would continue building on U.S. government practices of righting wrongs and providing redress for past government atrocities. In direct response to 246 years of slavery, Black Americans deserve reparations.
>
> I do not support the illogical arguments posed by some who say slavery happened over 100 years ago. It is not relevant today. Two of our most reverend and relevant guiding documents are the Declaration of Independence and the U.S. Constitution, both of which were created over 100 years ago. If those documents are important today, the same holds true for the sins of slavery.
>
> For almost 250 years, Black Americans were enslaved and forced to work without compensation, resulting in wealth creation for America and its White citizens. This act of barbarism against Blacks was the primary reason why the United States has become the economic leader it is today. This was the beginning of the wealth gap that plagues our country today.

The gap today between Black and White households is approximately $153,000, and this cavernous disparity continues to grow. If it is not closed, racial unrest will continue because the root cause of that unrest emanates from the poverty of Blacks intentionally created by the U.S. government.

Therefore, I am asking you to vote yes in support of H.R. 40, the bill submitted by Rep. Sheila Jackson Lee (D-Texas) on January 12, 2021. The 40 in the bill represents the 40 acres of land promised, but never transferred, to the four million Black people held in bondage until 1865. Financial reparations to the descendants of these tortured people are long overdue.

Thank you very much for reading my request to redress this atrocity. I look forward to learning about your affirmative vote on the reparations bill, H.R. 40. The passage of this legislation will be a huge step forward for our country.

Sincerely,
Your Constituent
[Your Name Here]

Notes

1. Miller, John W. "My Ancestor Owned 41 Slaves. What Do I Owe Their Descendants?" *America* magazine. November 28, 2018. https://www.america magazine.org/arts-culture/2018/11/28/my-ancestor-owned-41-slaves-what-do-i-owe-their-descendants

2. Sehgal, Kabir. "The Economics Behind Martin Luther King's 'I Have a Dream' Speech." *Fortune.* January 18, 2016. https://fortune.com/2016/01/18/martin-luther-king-i-have-a-dream/

3. Gopal, Keerti. "Generations of Pain: The Road to Reparations in Evanston." *Daily Northwestern.* May 29, 2020. https://dailynorthwestern.com/2020/05/29/city/generations-of-pain-the-road-to-reparations-in-evanston/

4. Eddy, Melissa. "For 60th Year, Germany Honors Duty to Pay Holocaust Victims." *New York Times.* November 17, 2012. https://www.nytimes.com/2012/11/18/world/europe/for-60th-year-germany-honors-duty-to-pay-holocaust-victims.html

5. Ibid.

6. McIntosh, Kristin, Emily Moss, Ryan Nunn, and Jay Shambaugh. "Examining the Black-white Wealth Gap." Brookings.edu. February 27, 2020. https://www.brookings.edu/blog/up-front/2020/02/27/examining-the-black-white-wealth-gap/

7. Wessler, Seth F. "Education Is Not Great Equalizer for Black Americans." NBC News. March 16, 2015. https://www.nbcnews.com/feature/in-plain-sight/wealth-moves-out-grasp-blacks-so-does-opportunity-n305196

8. Cohen, Patricia. "Racial Wealth Gap Persists Despite Degree, Study Says." *New York Times.* August 16, 2015. https://www.nytimes.com/2015/08/17/business/racial-wealth-gap-persists-despite-degree-study-says.html

9. "A Foretaste of Freedom." PBS. Accessed February 7, 2021. https://www.pbs.org/thisfarbyfaith/journey_2/p_9.html

10. "Negros of Savannah." Clipping from *New York-Daily Tribune.* February 13, 1865. http://www.freedmen.umd.edu/savmtg.htm

11. Foner, Eric. "First Chapter: Forever Free." *New York Times.* January 29, 2006. https://www.nytimes.com/2006/01/29/books/chapters/forever-free.html

12. Myers, Barton. "Sherman's Field Order No. 15." Texas Tech University. September 25, 2005. https://www.georgiaencyclopedia.org/articles/history-archaeology/shermans-field-order-no-15

13. Baradaran, Mehrsa. *The Color of Money.* Cambridge, MA, and London: Harvard University Press, 2018, p. 16.

14. "This Day in History: April 14, 1865: John Wilkes Booth Shoots Abraham Lincoln." History. Accessed February 7, 2021. https://www.history.com/this-day-in-history/john-wilkes-booth-shoots-abraham-lincoln

15. Reynolds, David S. "John Wilkes Booth and the Higher Law." *Atlantic.* April 12, 2015. https://www.theatlantic.com/politics/archive/2015/04/john-wilkes-booth-and-the-higher-law/385461/

16. Ibid.

17. Gates, Henry L., Jr. "The Truth Behind 40 Acres and a Mule." PBS. Accessed February 8, 2021. https://www.pbs.org/wnet/african-americans-many-rivers-to-cross/history/the-truth-behind-40-acres-and-a-mule/#:~:text=Andrew%20Johnson%2C%20Lincoln's%20successor%20and,had%20declared%20war%20on%20the

18. "President Johnson's Amnesty Proclamation." Library of Congress. Accessed February 8, 2021. https://www.loc.gov/resource/rbpe.23502500/?st=text

19. Click, Patricia C. "How Andrew Johnson Doomed the Roanoke Island Freedmen's Colony." *Slate*. November 8, 2017. https://slate.com/human-interest/2017/11/how-president-johnson-doomed-efforts-to-secure-land-for-former-slaves.html

20. Dorman, Travis. "Andrew Johnson, The Impeached President Who Wanted 'A White Man's Government.'" *Knoxville News Sentinel*. July 30, 2020. https://www.knoxnews.com/story/news/local/tennessee/2020/07/30/andrew-johnson-impeached-president-tennessee-history/5450438002/

21. Masur, Louis P. "How the South Rose Again." *American Scholar*. March 4, 2019. https://theamericanscholar.org/how-the-south-rose-again/

22. Guttman, Jon. "Did Slave Owners Receive Compensation for the Loss of Slaves?" History.net. Accessed February 9, 2021. https://www.historynet.com/did-slave-owners-receive-compensation-for-the-loss-of-slaves.htm

23. Khan, Imran. "Britain was Built on the Backs, and Souls, of Slaves." Al Jazeera. June 11, 2020. https://www.aljazeera.com/features/2020/6/11/britain-was-built-on-the-backs-and-souls-of-slaves

24. "Hawaiian Homes Commission Act." Department of Hawaiian Home Lands. Accessed February 10, 2021. https://dhhl.hawaii.gov/hhc/laws-and-rules/

25. Blakemore, Erin. "The Thorny History of Reparations in the United States." Library of Congress. https://www.history.com/news/reparations-slavery-native-americans-japanese-internment#:~:text=In%201946%2C%20Congress%20created%20the,to%20176%20tribes%20and%20bands

26. Ibid.

27. Jan, Tracy. "Reparations Mean More Than Money for Family Who Endured Slavery, Japanese American Internment." *Washington Post*. January 24, 2020. https://www.washingtonpost.com/graphics/2020/business/reparations-slavery-japanese-american-internment/

28. Qureshi, Bilal. "From Wrong to Right: A U.S. Apology for Japanese Internment." NPR. August 9, 2013. https://www.npr.org/sections/codeswitch/2013/08/09/210138278/japanese-internment-redress

29. Jan, Tracy. "Reparations Mean More Than Money For Family Who Endured Slavery, Japanese American Internment." *Washington Post*. January 24, 2020. https://www.washingtonpost.com/graphics/2020/business/reparations-slavery-japanese-american-internment/

30. "Mail Call: A Belated Apology." National WWII Museum. February 14, 2019. https://www.nationalww2museum.org/war/articles/mail-call-belated-apology#:~:text=Near%20the%20war's%20end%2C%20between,and%20homes%20to%20return%20to.

31. Lee, Sheila J. "H.R. 40 Is Not a Symbolic Act. It's a Path to Restorative Justice." ACLU. May 22, 2020. https://www.aclu.org/news/racial-justice/h-r-40-is-not-a-symbolic-act-its-a-path-to-restorative-justice/

32. Minardi, Margot. "Why Was Belinda's Petition Approved?" Royal House and Slave Quarters. Accessed February 10, 2021. https://royallhouse.org/why-was-belindas-petition-approved/#:~:text=For%20those%20slaves%20of%20Loyalist,that%20this%20policy%20be%20enforced.

33. "Reparations: Has the Time Finally Come?" ACLU Southern California. June 19, 2020. https://www.aclusocal.org/en/news/reparations-has-time-finally-come

34. "Congress Abolished the African Slave Trade." History.com. Accessed February 11, 2021. https://www.history.com/this-day-in-history/congress-abolishes-the-african-slave-trade

35. Little, Becky. "A Survivor of the Last Slave Ship Lived Until 1940." History.com. April 7, 2020. https://www.history.com/news/last-slave-ship-survivor-matilda-maccrear

36. Roper, Matt. "True Story Behind America's Last Slave and How Her Past Was Kept Family Secret." Mirror. March 27, 2020. https://www.mirror.co.uk/news/us-news/true-story-behind-americas-last-21769157

37. Reeves, Jay. "America's Last Slave Ship Could Offer a Case for Reparations." ABC News. October 5, 2019. https://abcnews.go.com/US/wireStory/americas-slave-ship-offer-case-reparations-66080792

38. Miller, John W. "My Ancestor Owned 41 Slaves: What Do I Owe Their Descendants?" America magazine. November 28, 2018. https://www.americamagazine.org/arts-culture/2018/11/28/my-ancestor-owned-41-slaves-what-do-i-owe-their-descendants

39. Gilreath, Ariel. "Unearthing the Past: Furman Reckons with Its Early Leadership." Greenville Journal. October 17, 2018. https://greenvillejournal.com/top-stories/unearthing-the-past-furman-reckons-with-its-early-leadership/

40. Furman, Felicia. "Interview with Felicia Furman." Reparations 4 Slavery. Accessed February 11, 2021. https://reparations4slavery.com/interview-with-felicia-furman/

41. Reilly, Lucas. "Robert Smalls: The Slave Who Stole a Confederate Ship and Became a Congressman." Mental Floss. February 12, 2019. https://www.mentalfloss.com/article/91630/robert-smalls-slave-who-stole-confederate-warship-and-became-congressman

42. Tom, Brittany. "The Descendants: Robert Smalls' Great-Great Grandson Says He's the Unsung Hero of the Civil War." Grio. February 21, 2013. https://thegrio.com/2013/02/21/the-descendants-robert-smalls-great-great-grandson-says-hes-the-unsung-hero-of-the-civil-war/

43. Oster, Lauren. "Behind the Address: The Inspiring Story of the Robert Smalls Home." HGTV. Accessed February 11, 2021. https://www.hgtv.com/design/home-tours/the-robert-smalls-home

44. Furman, Felicia. "Interview with Felicia Furman." Reparations 4 Slavery. Accessed February 11, 2021. https://reparations4slavery.com/interview-with-felicia-furman/

45. Miller, John W. "My Ancestor Owned 41 Slaves: What Do I Owe Their Descendants?" *America* magazine. November 28, 2018. https://www.americamagazine.org/arts-culture/2018/11/28/my-ancestor-owned-41-slaves-what-do-i-owe-their-descendants

46. Cohen, Seth. "Reparations Now: Why White People Must Join the Call to Pay Reparations for Slavery." *Forbes*. June 28, 2020. https://www.forbes.com/sites/sethcohen/2020/06/28/reparations-now/?sh=54b41bfb547e

47. Ibid

48. Innis, Charlie. "Durham Calls for Federal Reparations for the Descendants of Enslaved People." *News & Observer*. October 6, 2020. https://www.newsobserver.com/news/local/counties/durham-county/article246245235.html

49. Schlesinger, Jacob M. "Reparations to Black Americans for Slavery Gain New Attention." *Wall Street Journal*. June 26, 2020. https://www.wsj.com/articles/reparations-to-black-americans-for-slavery-gain-new-attention-11595685600

50. Brown, DeNeen L. "'Uncomfortable Truth': The Push for a Slavery Reparations Commission in Congress." *Washington Post*. February 10, 2021. https://www.washingtonpost.com/history/2021/02/10/reparations-slavery-congress-hearing-commission/

51. El-Mekki, Sharif. "A Marshall Plan for Black America Is the Only Way to Repay This Country's Moral Debt." *Philadelphia Inquirer*. December 4, 2020. https://www.inquirer.com/opinion/commentary/biden-election-black-voters-philadelphia-marshall-plan-black-america-20201204.html

52. Lockhart, P.R. "How Slavery Became America's First Big Business." Vox. August 16, 2019. https://www.vox.com/identities/2019/8/16/20806069/slavery-economy-capitalism-violence-cotton-edward-baptist

53. Gopal, Keerti. "Generations of Pain: The Road to Reparations in Evanston." *Daily Northwestern*. May 29, 2020. https://dailynorthwestern.com/2020/05/29/city/generations-of-pain-the-road-to-reparations-in-evanston/

54. Davis, Casper Andre, Jr. "What Happened to Mine? A History of Black Reparations in the United States." 2015. https://digitalcommons.bard.edu/cgi/viewcontent.cgi?article=1192&context=senproj_s2015

55. "H.R.40 - Commission to Study and Develop Reparation Proposals for African-Americans Act." Congress.gov. Accessed February 12, 2021. https://www.congress.gov/bill/116th-congress/house-bill/40

56. Neiman, Susan. "Germany Paid Holocaust Reparations: Will the U.S. Do the Same for Slavery?" *Los Angeles Times*. July 21, 2019. https://www.latimes.com/opinion/story/2019-07-19/reparations-germany-hr40-holocaust-slavery

Epilogue

In March 2020, Ethel Branch, the former attorney general of the Navajo Nation, did something wonderful. She began raising a $5,000 fund that would be used to buy food and water for elderly members of the Hopi and Navajo Native American communities. To her amazement, the fundraising was enormously successful. The Navajo & Hopi Families COVID-19 Relief Fund received donations of almost $18 million. One of the major donors, contributing $10 million, was MacKenzie Scott, the great philanthropist mentioned in Chapter 3. However, the most unlooked for and surprising donations came from citizens of Ireland. Yes, that island in northern Europe.

The catalyst for this response from the Irish, including $100,000 from Larry Mullen Jr., the drummer from the band U2, was a tweet about the fund from a reporter. The donations began to flow in immediately. More intriguingly, it was the accompanying remarks such as "we remember" and "for kindness shown to Ireland" that explained the reason behind the powerful response of the Irish. Many of the comments referred to the help provided to the Irish during the Great Famine of 1845 to 1852. Remarkably, in 1847, the Native American Choctaw people donated $170 to Ireland. So now, almost 175 years later, the Irish were displaying their gratitude. The most poignant statement that accompanied a donation was "we remember what your people did for us."[1]

It is this spirit of "paying it forward" that I am hopeful will be the result of this book. I am positively convinced that readers of *A Letter to My White Friends and Colleagues* will feel compelled to help the Black community and pay it forward for what our people did for America, not to mention making up for what our government did to us.

While I will not get effusively optimistic, for the first time in my six decades on this planet, I see glimmers of hope for Black people in America. There seems to be an announcement almost every day about a company or person doing something financially positive for the Black community. Whites are beginning to empathize with the horrible financial conditions of the Black community and act to share their wealth. There is evidence of such behavior in the sections of this book that discuss each one of my recommendations.

For example, over the past year, United Negro College Fund donations increased 300% as 159,000 new donors made contributions to HBCUs. "In memory of George Floyd" is often written on the checks.[2] In 2020, $1 billion was donated to HBCUs. This record-shattering amount of money directed to Black schools resulted in *Forbes* magazine calling 2020 "The Year of the HBCU."[3] But more important than that headline is the true positive impact of the actions. It can be explained best by a comment from Norfolk State University's president, Javaune Adams-Gaston, who said after receiving $40 million, "You can breathe a sigh of relief and focus on doing what we are here to do, which is to give our students an opportunity for excellence in the classroom and development on who they are going to be as leaders in the world."[4]

While the country desperately needs more Black-owned banks, the aforementioned record amount of money donated to HBCUs has been deposited. In fact, as reported in the *Wall Street Journal*, the second quarter of 2020 saw assets in Black-owned banks increase by 10%. This was the largest increase for Black banks from one quarter to the next in 20 years.[5]

The story of Black-owned businesses also has a sliver of sunshine amidst a storm of bad news. In the past year, due primarily to COVID-19, over 40% of Black-owned businesses have closed permanently. That is the largest percentage of closings by any racial or ethnic group. Yet at the same time that businesses were closing, new businesses were opening. From February to September 2020, the number of Black-owned businesses increased 2%, compared to 1% for Latino businesses, a decline of 1% for White-owned businesses, and a decline of 17% for Asian-owned businesses.[6]

On March 17, 2021, I awakened to a wonderful news headline: "This Major U.S Bank Just Endorsed Reparations for Black Americans."[7] The CNN article reported the encouraging story that Amalgamated Bank, the largest union-owned bank in the country, was the first American bank to endorse HR 40, the federal legislation focused on reparations.

All of these recent examples of positive support for the Black community are great signs of help, signifying that a change may be in the wind. Now, if true and meaningful change is to occur, we must foster this momentum so that it continues, with exponential growth annually.

In the next 75 years, when readers of this book have gone to heaven, we will meet the ancestors who were enslaved. They will likely ask, "What did you do to help my descendants once they were free?" Hopefully, your answer will be, "I helped the Black community by sharing my wealth. I donated to HBCUs, I spent part of my annual budget with Black-owned businesses, and I deposited money into Black-owned banks. I am also proud to tell you that I wrote letters to the government, imploring them to do what is right by giving monetary reparations to your descendants as partial payment for the work that you and other ancestors were forced to do without compensation!"

Notes

1. Mineo, Liz. "Making Gifts That Keep on Giving." *Harvard Gazette*. March 12, 2021. https://news.harvard.edu/gazette/story/2021/03/a-modest-plan-to-help-native-elders-amid-covid-draws-18m/
2. Winfield, Kristen. "Bigger Than Money: NBA All-Star Donations to HBCUs Just the Icing on the Cake." *Daily News*. March 6, 2021. https://www.nydailynews.com/sports/basketball/ny-nba-hbcu-all-star-game-20210306-ko33sjuprjaaxfhmqlox673gka-story.html
3. Nietzel, Michael, T. "Four Reasons Why 2020 Was the Year of the HBCU." Forbes. January 2, 2021. https://www.forbes.com/sites/michaeltnietzel/2021/01/02/four-reasons-why-2020-was-the-year-of-the-hbcu/?sh=424b6bf14f50
4. Bunn, Curtis. "From Covid Aid to Record Donations: Influx of Funding Helps Keep HBCUs' Doors Open." NBC News. February 19, 2021. https://www.nbcnews.com/news/nbcblk/covid-aid-record-donations-influx-funding-helps-keep-hbcus-doors-n1258357
5. Burton, Amber, Justin Scheck, and John West. "The Battle to Keep America's Black Banks Alive." *Wall Street Journal*. November 16, 2020. https://www.wsj.com/articles/the-battle-to-keep-americas-black-banks-alive-11604725200
6. Sasso, Michael. "U.S. Black-Owned Firms Make Surprise Comeback to Pre-Covid Level." *Washington Post*. October 29, 2020. https://www.washingtonpost.com/business/on-small-business/us-black-owned-firms-make-surprise-comeback-to-pre-covid-level/2020/10/28/be1e3100-194b-11eb-8bda-814ca56e138b_story.html
7. Maruf, Ramishah. "This Major U.S Bank Just Endorsed Reparations for Black Americans." CNN. March 17, 2021. https://www.cnn.com/2021/03/17/business/amalgamated-bank-hr-40/index.html

Discussion Questions

When a young White woman asked Malcolm X, "What can I do to help?" following a college tour speech in 1960, he replied, "Nothing." Why do you think this was this his initial response?

In what ways has the U.S. government supported the creation of the Black/White wealth gap? What issues has the wealth gap caused? How can White people help close that gap in America?

The author describes himself as a race man. What is a race man/woman? Is it possible for a White person to be a race man/woman?

What role does philanthropy play in closing the Black/White wealth gap? What were the three main contributions to the Black/White wealth gap?

How has the government explicitly discriminated against Blacks historically? What industries benefitted from slavery?

Originally, the primary mission of HBCUs was to teach and pre-pare formerly enslaved and free Black people the skills for gainful employment. What impact would the closing of HBCUs have on the Black community today?

What have been the challenges faced by Black banks? Why have Black banks not been as successful as White immigrant banks, like Bank of Italy? What is the importance of Black banks today?

Why are Black-owned businesses important to the Black community? What the primary challenges to the growth of Black-owned business?

Do you agree that White people have a responsibility to bank with Black banks as a way to support the Black community? Please explain why.

Should reparations go to the descendants of people enslaved? Why or why not?

How can reparations help to close the Black/White wealth gap? Do reparations work?

Acknowledgments

AFTER I RETIRED in 2019, I never expected to write another book. Then, on June 23, 2020, my retirement plans changed. An editor from the publishing company John Wiley & Sons reached out to me, about a month after George Floyd was murdered. The country was exploding with protests and civil unrest in response to the murder of Floyd and several other Black people by the police. Blacks across the country were stating emphatically that we have had enough of this terroristic mistreatment. And, for the first time in my 63-year-life, a significant portion of the country's White population was showing empathy that went beyond words. Many were asking, "What can I do to help Black people?"

I suspect that is the question that led the Wiley editor to me, with an invitation to write this book. After saying yes to the offer, I assembled a trio of brilliant people to work with me. As a result of their phenomenal work ethic and commitment, I believe we have produced something special. Accordingly, I would like to give them special acknowledgment. They are Kevin Ozenne, the husband of Susan and the father of Ava; Garry Hutchinson, the husband of Bernice and the father of Alexandra; and Darlene Le, the daughter of Trang and Vuong.

I would also like to give thanks to the two women who are the most important people in my life, my daughters Akilah Naeem and Ariel Naillah, two bright, beautiful, selfless, and kind women.

My brother Johnnie and my Uncle Ray are the two most important men in my life and to them I say thank you.

I also have a wide orbit of people who are not related by blood, but I would be remiss if I did not give thanks and appreciation to them. These friends are the best! They took time out of their busy schedules to read chapters, give me written feedback, and offer sage advice. I am blessed to have them as friends. So, thanks to Gil (my best friend), Mike, Bincey, John, Ray, Dawn, Ms. Barbara, Larry, Andy, Brenda, Mindy, Jeff, Henry, Jackie, Paul, Sheelah, Matt, Kristine, Aaron, Pat, Donna, Roza, Marissa, Nicole, Susan, Charles, and my attorneys Lisa and Jennifer.

The Wiley team was outstanding also, and I would like to thank them. They are Sally, Emilia, Rhea, Amy, Michael, Dawn, Alyssa, and Shannon.

Finally, I must acknowledge Jeanenne Ray, the editor at Wiley who reached out to me last summer. From her research, she discovered that I am a Black "race man." She believed it was important to provide a platform for my voice to support the Black community. The following statement about working with me demonstrates her commitment to helping the Black community: "This is important . . . perhaps it will be the most important project I will have worked on in my career." Thank you, Jeanenne.

About the Author

STEVEN ROGERS retired from Harvard Business School in 2019 where he was the "MBA Class of 1957 Senior Lecturer" in General Management. He taught entrepreneurial finance and his own course, "Black Business Leaders and Entrepreneurship." Prior to HBS, Professor Rogers taught in the MBA and PhD programs at the Kellogg School of Management at Northwestern University, where he received the Outstanding Professor Award for the Executive MBA Program 26 times and the daytime program twice.

More recently, Rogers joined the Steans Family Foundation as an advisor to develop an economic plan for a poverty-stricken Black community in Chicago. In 2020, he toured 10 HBCUs, where he taught a workshop titled "Entrepreneurial Finance for Black Entrepreneurs." He has also served on the board of directors of several corporations.

Named one of the top 150 influential people in America by *Ebony* magazine, Rogers is the author of *The Entrepreneur's Guide to Finance and Business* and of multiple Harvard Business School case studies, as well as podcasts focused on Black business and financial issues.

Index